FOREWORD

Dr. Robert Schuller
Pastor - The Crystal Cathedral

Success truly is within the reach of everyone.
Paul and Dan's book, Why Not Me?,
gives you both simple rules and applications
to see the possibilities in life
and open the door to true wealth.
It is practical, touching, and full of real life
'Possibility Thinkers'.

Go for it; you'll be glad you did.
They made it big as teenagers;
if they could, you can too.

"A concise book weaving metaphor with eternal truths about how to consciously create success. Easy to read, leading you to re-discover your own inner wisdom."

Lee Pulos, Ph.D.
Clinical Psychologist

"The Monaghans have written a sure-fire guide to success. They know the keys to success are simplicity itself, because they have gone the route."

Burke Hedges
Author, *Who Stole The American Dream?*

"To realize your fondest dreams and exceed your highest aspirations, read, learn, understand, and apply the timeless principles in Why Not Me? This book will help many achieve financial and personal independence. I love the book and its authors, who live and demonstrate the vital, vibrant truths they write and teach."

Mark Victor Hansen
Author, *Dare To Win*

3 4 5 7 8
6 9 8

WHY NOT ME?

9
Principles
to Open a
World
of Wealth

PAUL & DAN MONAGHAN

PRIME
BOOKS
INCORPORATED

Canadian Cataloguing in Publication Data
Main entry under title:

Monaghan, Dan.
 Why not me?

ISBN 1-895250-54-4

1. Success. 2. Success in business.
I. Monaghan, Paul. II. Title.

BF637.S8M6 1992   158   C92-093894-9

Printed in Canada

Cover design by ACP Associates Inc., Markham, Ontario

Destiny Seminars Inc.
276 Kingsbury Square, Suite 104
Lake Tahoe, Nevada, U.S.A. 89449
1-800-663-7326

Contents

Fable   11
Preface   25

Principle #1
  Program Yourself For Success   31

Principle #2
  Practice Perspective   45

Principle #3
  The Inversarian Principle   59

Principle #4
  Create A Wonderful Self-Esteem   65

Principle #5
  Make Your Dreams Come True   79

Principle #6
  Create Your Own Declarations   123

Principle #7
  Discover The Power of Association   141

Principle #8
  Accept Responsibility   151

Principle #9
  The Master Principle   163

*We dedicate this book
to our loving and supportive parents
who gave us the freedom
to find our way
and who inspired us
with their never-ending belief.*

The
9
Principles
to Open
A
World of
Wealth

A Fable

"Master, hey master come quick", screamed Eric the peasant boy. He was a servant at the Martinol castle. "Hurry, hurry, something terrible, oh so terrible!" he cried. Michael was by the pond fishing and pondering the good fortune of his life. Those thoughts had vanished now. Instead, young Michael was frightened by the look of horror on the peasant's face. Something serious has happened. "What is it? What's the matter?", Michael demanded.

Just then, the boy fell unconscious from exhaustion and sheer panic. Michael, the only son in the Martinol family, sensed a deep feeling inside. He didn't know what was the matter, only that something definitely wasn't right. He could have never been prepared for what he was about to experience.

He arrived at the massive stone castle within five or six minutes. The castle was over 200 years old. It was the residence of Duke Martinol and his family. Practically everyone in the little village of Westinshire was gathered around the entrance of the castle.

The Martinol's were loved by everyone in the village. They had created work and charities to benefit almost all of them in some way. When he made his way through the crowd, Michael noticed tears on everyone's face. It could only mean one thing. The Duke was dead!

Michael could hardly contain the pain he felt as he held his father whom he loved so much. "Why did he die so young?" he cried. "I need my father. Oh, why, why, why?"

Michael cried tears that were different from any others he had shed. These tears hurt. They seemed to come from the pit of his stomach. They didn't stop either. These were aching tears, tears he had never known before.

The vicar had wonderful words for those gathered behind the church at the burial site. Michael and his mother remembered coming to Westinshire. They remembered how the Duke gave away much of his riches to the people of the village. That might explain why they were all present at the cemetery.

The Duke was the perfect father to Michael. He loved his son and always provided an ideal environment for him. They played by the brook, they ran in the fields of England, and travelled by coach to visit relatives in Scotland. Life would be very different for Michael now.

A few days after the funeral, Michael's mother asked if she could discuss something with him. By this time, Michael was beginning to think what he would do with the fortunes he would receive as inheritance. His father was enormously wealthy. He had more money than anyone even imagined.

It was a local custom that the eldest son receive the proceeds from the estate at the time of death of his father. Not a consolation at all, but those thoughts of instant wealth helped Michael pass the time and ease the pain a little.

"Michael, you are entitled to all your father's riches right now," explained his mother. The young man had thoughts, somewhat selfish thoughts, of the wealth he was about to receive. It didn't take him long to mentally spend all that money. It may be strange, considering he just lost his father, but Michael became excited about money. He began rattling off ways in which he would spend the inheritance.

"Not so fast son. Several years ago, your father prepared something for you to read on the occasion of his death. Perhaps you should read it before you make any further plans."

The Scroll

She handed him a parchment scroll with a gold ribbon and family wax seal. Michael opened it slowly and tears began to stream down his cheeks. The scroll was entitled, My Parting Words Dear Son. He read on...

Dearest Michael, my only child,
the apple of my eye:

> This letter was to be sealed until my death. This is a terrible time for you and your mother, I know. Michael, know that I have had a full life, that you have brought me more sunshine than one man deserves. You have caused me to change the course of my life and to be totally fulfilled. Both your mother and I thanked God often for you, Michael.

> It's my sincere hope that I have passed unto you all that you will need to live a free, happy, and rewarding life, a life similar to the one I have lived. My son, I must make yet one more request from you. I am no longer here with you, to be by your side when life's storms hit. I need to teach you my final lesson.

The lesson is simple. Once you learn it, a world of wealth, happiness, and joy will be yours forever. I trust you Michael.

The reason I have decided to follow this path for your final lesson is that I wanted to teach you what I learned as a young man. Michael, we have never really spoken much about my youth. I was not always wealthy. How I became financially secure was by apprenticing under a master of success, Baron Westin. While others followed the path of the masses, I persisted with my teacher.

I was born a poor child, my father was a pauper. He was the town drunk; the court jester. As a boy, I would often observe the Baron as his shiny, jewelled coach would come to our village. I imagined what it would be like to live the life the Baron lived.

As I grew older, I would hear the negativity and complaints about Baron Westin from the town folks. I could never understand why they were so mean to him. He was such a loving, warm-hearted man.

When I was 14, I took a job working as his servant in his chamber. He took a liking to me and we became quite fond of one another. I knew he knew something about life that I didn't know. While pondering the life the Baron lived, I began wondering if I could be so fortunate. I asked myself, "Why Not Me?", "Why couldn't I learn the things the Baron learned and thus profit so, as he had?" Those questions would not rest until they were answered.

One day, I posed a similar question to Baron Westin. "All you had to do was ask." he replied. He shared with me the 9 principles to success in life. I set out to acquire the principles and apply them to my life. It has been an interesting journey.

These are your instructions: Unlock my treasure chest of wealth. Once you have opened this treasure chest, my dearest

Michael, you will know, you will just know about true wealth. As you begin on this journey, which might not be easy, remember the world's four most powerful words:

Choice

You have choice in this life, Michael. Don't ever think you don't. Life is made up of choices. Choose wisely my son. I have led you through some of those tough choices. You have made me proud.

Some people think they have no choice in life because of their circumstances. They think they are without choice because of condition of existence, heredity, or environments. Don't count yourself among them son. No, you always have choice. Never forget choice. You can always choose the best.

Responsibility

Some unfortunates are always quick to point a finger to others as the cause of their pitiful lives. You know better than to ever do that, Michael. In life, remember to always stand tall in the face of whatever life brings your way. Take responsibility for your actions and decisions.

Change

Refuse to be stagnant, my son. When the masses are stifled, stand apart by refusing to accept conformity. Be a friend to flexibility and change. If something in life is not working for you, change it. Change is good and desirable, Michael, despite what others may say.

Think of how many of our great institutions have all but died because they refused to budge. "It's the way we have always done it," they say. Think of the ideas which have met with sudden peril because of the closed minds of those unwilling to change.

Determination

Be steadfast with determination son, even in the face of life's obstacles. These challenges of life are essential for your future achievement.

Determination is breaking down a seemingly impossible task by concentrating on what is achievable. Stay on target, refuse to give up, and proceed to create what you want in life. I see in you a potential to change the world. Your job is to use that potential to change it for the better, never the worse.

Be of good cheer, young man. I am close by. Learn your lessons, my son, and all will be well.

Farewell

Your loving father

By this time, Michael was weeping openly. He cherished his father's words. What a lesson to learn. Even though Michael thought he had received his father's final lesson, in reality, it had barely begun.

His mother handed him a key to the small rosewood box that sat on the mantle above the fireplace. It had always been there. Michael never really paid any attention to it before. He placed the key in the keyhole with anticipation. He turned it, and inside, strangely enough, he found another key. This one was an elaborate, large, gold key. He removed it and shut the cover to the small box. As he did, strange things began to occur.

The room seemed to shift. The whole fireplace began to rotate. Michael was amazed at what he saw. The fireplace rotated to reveal a concealed room. The room was opulent. It was not furnished but had as its centre piece a huge solid gold treasure chest. Michael's heart began to pound with excitement. He had always wondered where his father had stored his vast wealth. This chest must be the place!

His mind raced as he placed the gold key into the great chest. He had visions of diamonds, pearls, silver, precious gems, and massive amounts of gold. It took some effort for Michael to even lift the top off the chest. What would be inside? How much would all this be worth? What would he do with the treasure contained herein?

Michael could never have imagined what he was about to discover. He could never have prepared for the shock he was about to face. As he looked inside, his heart seemed to stop. His eyes fell, his spirit sunk. The massive golden treasure chest was empty; empty, except for what seemed like an old, ratty, worn-out book, covered in dust.

The Book

The book was handwritten by his father and entitled simply, *Nine Principles* . "What could this mean?" he wondered. "How could my father do this to me?" He was not the least bit impressed. "Where is my money?" His disappointment quickly turned to anger. "What was the point of all this?" Michael could not understand the meaning of this old, dusty book being in the chest which supposedly housed his father's massive riches. This day was truly a disappointment for Michael.

He reasoned that the answer to all these questions must be contained within this book. He picked it up and began to read from its fragile pages. It began... "To the man who dares to read this book, be ye forewarned... you are about to become one the world's truly wealthy people." The book had a strange sort of grip on him. He couldn't put it down. It gained his attention right from the start and did not let go until the book was read in its entirety. Many hours had passed until he turned to the last page. It was almost dawn before he came to the last page. Sure enough, his father was right. His father had predicted that he would know, he would just know. Well, now he did know.

He knew for sure about the world of wealth. His eyes were open for the first time. His disappointment began to turn to joy and excitement. He understood so much more about life. He understood about the differences between the masses and the few who became truly successful. Michael knew that luck, heritage, blessing, giftedness had little to do with true success. Michael would never be the same. He was changed forever.

The sun was just rising while Michael walked alone near the meadow. A world he had never seen before surrounded him. The dew on the grass brushed his shoes. The birds sang sweeter than ever before. The flowers and trees were different, more colorful and vibrant now. The air felt fresher. Even the apple he ate from the orchard tasted differently to him. Michael's world would never be the same. His whole world had come alive. Everything made sense to him now.

He reflected on the lessons he had just learned, and as he sat by the brook, he penned a letter to his dearly departed father.

Dear Father

Some people are blessed with good parents, others have magnificent parents; I have been blessed with the most blessed of parents.

Go, dear father, to your eternal rest knowing that you have made a man of me. You could have given me a fish, yet you chose to teach me to fish for myself.

You have taught me so well that I have decided to give all my new wealth to the poor. I will open my own world of wealth by using the 9 Principles. Baron Westin did it, you have done it, so why not me?

Love, your dear son

Michael decided to give everything away and start from where his father began. He knew that his world would open exactly like he wanted. He now had the 9 Principles to open a world of wealth.

Now it's your turn ...

These principles have always existed,
and were passed down through the ages
to those who have wanted to listen.
They have been passed down
through the ages
to great minds and leaders,
more recently to such notables as Lincoln,
Franklin, Ford, Edison,
Churchill, and Emerson.
In the last few decades,
the Principles here have been heralded
by such people as Napoleon Hill,
Martin Luther King,
Norman Vincent Peale,
Og Mandino, Robert Schuller, and others.
They have been passed on
to the great success minds of today,
and searched out
by those who wanted to listen,
people like Dan and Paul Monaghan.

- *Preface*
-
-
-
-
-
- **BY**
- **DAN AND PAUL**
- **MONAGHAN**
-
-
-
-
-
-

Hi, we're Paul and Dan Monaghan. We have opened our own world of wealth; mentally, emotionally, spiritually, financially, and socially. Our story, heard by countless thousands across the world, speaks of two brothers who, despite our age, created a multi-million dollar business in a short time.

We have said that the quality of your life is dependant often on the quality of the questions you ask. Well, *Why Not Me?* may be one of the most powerful questions you will ever ask yourself.

We have come from simple roots—our father was a custodian and our mother a part-time nurse. Without any formal education or business experience (except delivering pizza), we achieved incredible results in a very short period of time.

What if...

Picture yourself writing a check for $10,000 and see yourself doing so without giving any thought about whether you have the funds to cover the check. Of course you do! Now, visualize yourself driving down the California Pacific Coast highway, the sun shining through the sunroof in your very own, brand new Mercedes Benz. You are off to meet some important people for lunch at the Ritz-Carlton. You feel confident because you're happy to be who you are. You are living the good life. You are wearing a designer outfit that fits you perfectly and makes you look like a million dollars. You are a millionaire. You finally have the things you want in life.

Really let your mind get into this. Imagine yourself doing the things you really want to do in life. You decide that working at the J.O.B. (Just Over Broke) is not what you want anymore. You decide to make your dreams come true. You get an opportunity to make a lot of money doing your hobby. Everyone has something they would gladly do for free.

You feel like you're in heaven because you see yourself actually making an incredible living doing just that. Wonderful! You choose when to work and when to play. Speaking of playing, it's something you do a lot of these days.

You see yourself taking more vacations in one year than most people take in their lifetime. Money is not a problem, so first-class travel is the way you go. Always! You stay only at five-star hotels. You reflect how great it feels that you can now enjoy yourself like this. You laugh because today, you are a generous tipper and you enjoy doing it. You really get a kick out of watching the waiter's face when they see the size of your generosity.

You are invited to all the charity events. See yourself signing a donation for $50,000 to your favorite charity. Imagine being invited to be a member of the Board of Directors. People know you as a warm-hearted, kind person. Not pretentious, very real and very happy.

See now what's going on for you mentally? You go to sleep and you are at total peace with yourself. You now have what you have always longed for—calmness of mind. You are at peace in your own skin. You feel lovable and capable. You know that you matter to yourself and to your family. The world is a wonderful place for you. You value each moment.

You have total confidence and total faith. Imagine how proud you feel when people are speaking about how much they like you and how much they like being around you. You are a wonderful person, and today, you are in a perfect spot in life. Imagine being perfectly healthy emotionally.

Laughter is the main ingredient in your life. You are having fun. Your life is full of passion. You are hot and you know it. It seems that everything you touch turns to gold. Your world is the way you have designed it. You feel great and it shows.

This might feel like a fantasy for you today, but remember that everything on the planet started off as a fantasy. Fantasy is a good thing. The good news is that the book you now hold in your hands will show you specifically how to turn that fantasy into reality. You can live beyond your present limits. You can easily live the situation we just described, and more.

This book will show you how to do it. It's easier than you might imagine. It's so much better to live it than to fantasize about it. Even if your fantasy is considerably different from the picture we painted above, this book is designed to help you live the life *you* desire. If you know what you want, this book **will** show you how to receive it. Fast!

This book is about wealth. But it's not limited to money. True wealth involves so much more than dollars and cents. *Why Not Me?* is about being wealthy in your happiness, in your relationships. It's about having untold mental riches. It's about having the calmness of mind that we all want. It's also about being the kind of person you want to become. It's doing the things you want to do. It's about living your potential.

What do Michelangelo, Einstein, Edison, Ford, Columbus all have in common? They were labelled, at one time in their life, as being incompetent. People thought they were retarded, deluded, and dumb. They suffered from false limitations placed upon them by others. They were treated unfairly, criticised, ridiculed, and even punished for their thoughts. Do you know anyone like this? Know anyone specifically? Someone real close to you? Take heart. If you are being ridiculed, criticized, or lambasted for your beliefs, then you are on the right track. This book will show you why and how to go against the crowd with confidence and live what we call *The Inversarian Lifestyle.*

We began as teenagers asking *Why Not Me* questions. As a result, we opened our own world of wealth. We want to share with you what worked for us. We want to share with you the 9 principles we used to unlock our own potential. Why 9 principles? Through our research of the lives of super successful individuals we found a pattern of principles for high achievement. We examined why we had achieved what we had in such a short period of time and at such a young age, and these 9 principles were the most powerful things we learned and incorporated into our lives. They worked for us, and they'll work for you.

If you think that the government will look after you and take care of you, you are sadly mistaken. The truth is only you can be responsible for you. People trust in their companies to provide security. There is no such thing as security. It's a myth! Just speak to someone who has given a corporation 23 of the best years of their life and are thrown out on the street because of declining profits.

There is no security but the security you create within yourself.

People are deceived into believing that education will be the ticket to wealth. If that were the case, college professors would be wealthy. We hardly find any wealthy educators. If educators knew so much about creating wealth, why aren't more of them rich?

People think that in order to win, you must have good luck, inherit money, be born with massive talent, and other fallacies. The way to true riches is to assume the responsibility for your own destiny. Bet on yourself! You are worth it.

Just ask yourself ...

WHY
NOT
ME?

- *Principle #1*
-
-
- PROGRAM YOURSELF FOR SUCCESS
-
-
-
- **THE PATHWAY TO FREEDOM—THE MIND**
-
-
- *"If you think your thought is powerful,*
- *your thought IS powerful."*
-                                    Thomas Troward
-
-
-

You have been born with the most sophisticated and complex instrument the planet has ever known—your marvelous mind. Very few people have any concept of what the mind actually is like, how to describe it, or how to alter it forever.

We were not born with a manual on what the mind is or how to maximize its use. Without this information, thousands of people wander through the deserted halls of dreams, always hoping but rarely achieving.

We have discovered probably the best concept in the world today to describe the mind, how it works, and how to change it. The beauty of this model is that it is not difficult to understand.

The Stickperson concept was developed in the 1930's by Dr. Thruman Fleet, the founder of *Concept Therapy*. He discovered that your mind can be divided into 3 distinct parts. Your Conscious Mind (Part 1), your Subconscious mind (Part 2), and your Body (Part 3). Since we tend to think in pictures, Fleet invented a picture of the mind.

"Lack and limitation can only exist when we make room for them in our mind. You become what you think about. Everything we have or do is preceded by an image in our mind."

The Stickperson

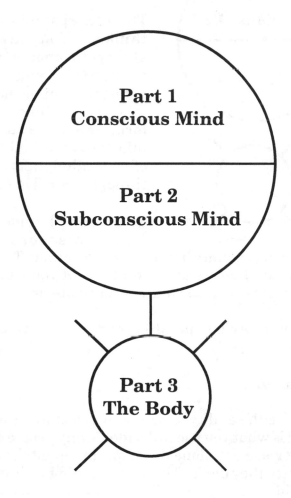

Part 1
Conscious Mind

Part 2
Subconscious Mind

Part 3
The Body

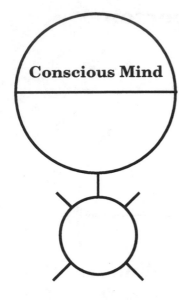

Conscious Mind

Part 1
The Conscious Mind

This is the part of you that thinks. You have the ability to choose which thoughts you will entertain. This is the place where ideas are formulated. You bring information into this part of your mind, information through your five senses.

Your free will resides here. Pain, pleasure, and limitation originate in the conscious mind. This part of your mind serves as a filter to what you will allow to be impressed into your subconscious mind.

The conscious mind is made up of six mental muscles.

• Reason

You have the ability to accept or reject any thought; reason is what you use to decide. Many people choose to never use, let alone develop, this mental muscle. It's a pity they don't. The world would be different if they did.

- **Imagination**

There is a power flowing into you which allows you to create big ideas. The power of your imagination is more powerful than all the nuclear power present in the world today. This is probably one of the most under used tools we have at our disposal; the ability to dream.

- **Will**

This is the muscle that allows you to concentrate. Most people are so easily taken off course because they have never developed this muscle. You have the power to mentally focus on your goals and never be taken off track because of your current circumstances, environment, or situation.

- **Intuition**

This is often referred to as your sixth sense. This is an actual mental faculty. You have the ability to pick up information through your intuition in a way that is unexplainable by modern science.

- **Memory**

You have a perfect memory. You never forget anything. You may need training as to how to retrieve it through your conscious mind, but it is perfect.

• Perception

You can develop your ability to view your world differently. You can decide how circumstances will affect your life. You can develop better ways to perceive your reality.

Imagine that you came home one afternoon and found your front lawn littered with garbage. If you are like most of us, chances are that would probably upset you, but you would clean it up. During the clean-up; you might wonder, "who on earth would want to do such a disgusting thing?"

Now the following afternoon, you come home and find that your front lawn is again littered with another truck-load of garbage. You'd be twice as angry as you were the evening before, but you would probably clean it up again, and again be wondering "Why would anyone want to do something like this?"

The third afternoon, you come home and the front lawn is again littered with garbage. This time you have had enough. You would vow to put a stop to such destruction and aggravation. You would take whatever measures are necessary to stop the insanity.

Now, think of all the garbage that is littered on the greatest front lawn in the world—your mind. Most people allow garbage to be dumped into their mind and refuse to do anything about it. The garbage we are talking about is negative thinking. If we are not careful, it's easy to allow others to pollute our mind.

You have a guard watching the *front lawn* of your mind. It's called reason. You can use your reason to accept or reject any ideas. You must not allow yourself to suffer from *stinkin' thinkin'*. Be sure your guard is always on duty. You are responsible to ensure he does his job.

You become what you
consciously think about.
Earl Nightingale

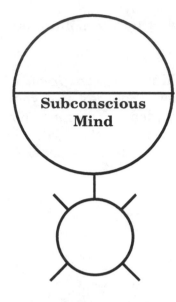

Subconscious
Mind

Part 2
The Subconscious Mind

This part of you is certainly the most magnificent. It is your power centre. Every thought your conscious mind chooses to accept, this part must willingly accept. It has no ability to reject it.

For every idea that your conscious mind conceives, your subconscious mind will create whatever is necessary to fulfil that picture. If you have pictures of poverty in your conscious mind, your subconscious mind will create in reality for you exactly that, right on schedule.

All your prior conditioning from parents, teachers, authority figures are found here. Whatever is impressed in this side of your personality will be expressed through the only medium it can, your body.

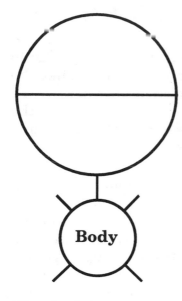

Part 3
Tho Body

This part of you is by far the smallest part of who you are. This part is the part that expresses what is happening on the inside. Your body never lies.

Whatsoever is impressed on your mind will express itself on the physical plain through your body.

Your body is an instrument of the mind; it materializes the exact pictures that are impressed on the mind. This involves behavior. Behavior and actions determine results. Want better results? Change your behaviors. Want better behaviors? Change the pictures in your subconscious mind. How do you do that? Change the pictures in your conscious mind.

You either choose your thoughts or accept them from an outside source. These thoughts develop into images or ideas in your conscious mind. You then impress the images upon your subconscious mind causing feelings. The feelings cause actions and the actions cause results.

39

The Farmer's Field

The conscious mind is like a farmer deciding what to plant in his field. The subconscious mind is like the farmers field. It has no choice as to what will be planted. When the farmer plants a corn seed, the field reaps corn. When the farmer plants a dandelion seed from the field, he will reap a dandelion.

Precisely how this works cannot be explained by science even today, but we do know the law exists. It would be foolish to think that by planting a dandelion seed, a stalk of corn would emerge from the ground, yet many people believe that this will happen in their lives. When you think a negative thought or concentrate on visions of failure, the results for you will be failure.

You decide which seeds you will plant by the thoughts you think. It is no more possible for a farmer to plant a dandelion seed and harvest corn than it is for you to think negative thoughts and reap positive results. Some people have been careless in what they have planted over the years, and now they have a field overrun by weeds. It will take a little time to clear the field. Start planting corn right away and soon you will have a rich, bountiful harvest.

We have no idea how the forces of nature turn an acorn into an oak tree, but we believe it will. Your subconscious mind utilizes all of the forces of nature to produce results.

It is no more difficult to plant a seed of corn than it is to plant a weed seed. The subconscious is the servant of man; learn how to use it by giving it commands which will produce the results you want.

Begin by asking a number of questions. The quality of your life is greatly determined by the quality of questions you ask. Start to think more effectively. Use the following questions to get the ball rolling:

❑ Why do so many people live paycheck to paycheck?

❑ Why do so many of your friends hate their jobs?

❑ Why do they keep promising to improve their lives, yet never do?

❑ Why do so many people seem to oppose your efforts to improve yourself?

❑ What have winners done to improve their thinking?

A friend of ours named Sarah discovered that she had embedded within her marvellous mind, ideas which were not her own. She set out to uncover her conditioning which had been governing her life, almost without her even knowing it. She was surprised that she had many beliefs which she no longer would espouse.

41

Over and over, Sarah heard things like:

> *Money doesn't grow on trees.*
> *We're poor but we are honest.*
> *Children should be seen and not heard.*
> *Play it safe.*
> *It's better to be safe than sorry.*

Without even realizing it, she still worried about money, because after all, *it didn't grow on trees.* She was sold the idea that poverty was a virtue, that children should keep their mouths shut, and that going the *safe* route in life was best. When she started thinking about it, she realized that those ideas were firmly embedded into her subconscious mind. She knew for her to grow, she would have to overcome the fixed ideas in her mind which were put there by her authority figures when she was only a child.

She knew that for her to change, she would need to change the pictures in her mind and get emotionally involved with new ones. She found out pretty quickly that messing with her conditioning was most uncomfortable. She knew she would have to endure if she was to see lasting changes. She is so much better off for having done so.

As you can see, we can have, do, or be anything we want. The only limitations are those we impose on ourselves through our thoughts.

"As a man thinks, so is he.
As he continues to think,
so he remains.
Man thus, in a measure,
becomes a servant
of his thoughts,
and through his thoughts,
he works out his affairs."

Bobby Charlton
Master Motivator

- *Principle #2*
-
-
- PRACTICE PERSPECTIVE
-
-
-
-
- **HOW TO SEE YOUR WORLD DIFFERENTLY**
-
-
- *"Don't sweat the small stuff.*
- *Remember, it's all small stuff."*
-
-
-
-

Practice perspective by changing the way you interpret your circumstance, situations, and environments. "The task is not to see a new world but to see the world with new eyes." The person who can change the way they view their world will win without fail.

John Milton said, "The mind in itself, in its own place, can make a hell out of heaven and heaven out of hell." You will experience in life the results of the dominant thoughts within your mind.

A stranger chanced upon several workers in a small town in Italy. Curious and interested, he began to inquire from the workers as to what they were doing. "I'm laying bricks", said the first worker. After a few minutes of idle chat, he asked of another, "What are you doing?" he continued, "Laying bricks, eh?" The other worker, somewhat indignantly responded, with shoulders straight and firmness of voice, "Laying bricks? No, sir. I am building a cathedral." Both workers were working on the same job. One saw his tasks as laying brick upon brick upon brick, while the other one saw a work being offered to the Glory of God.

Two people—two perspectives! Why is it that some people choose to see the worst in a situation while others choose to see the best in the same situation? Why do some people constantly see what's gone wrong while others look for what's right? Which one do you think will succeed further on this great journey we're on?

Everyone has obstacles. Everyone needs perspective in the face of those challenges. Your response to dealing with the storms of life will dictate the results you achieve. What follows is practical solutions to dealing with those times in life when everything seems to be going the opposite to your preferences.

Put Your Problems In Perspective

Remember...

... THERE IS SOMETHING
TO LEARN IN
EVERY PROBLEM.

Challenges of life will come. The only place on earth that we know of where there are no problems is a cemetery. Everywhere else will be hit by the storms of life. If you remember that there is something to learn in every problem, then you can learn to grow by the storms rather than being crushed by them.

W. Mitchell said, "It's not what happens to us that counts, it's what happens in us." He was right and he should know. His story of courage in becoming a serious burn victim and subsequent plane crash casualty which left him paralysed is an inspiration of someone who has sought to become better through adversity. Mitchell is probably one of the most *up* people on the planet, largely due to the lessons he learned about life and how to live it while recuperating from his injuries.

When I (Paul) was 15, I was devastated by the loss of almost all my friends. Something caused me to believe that I was inferior to my peers. No one liked me, so I thought. I created my own reality. I became an outcast, a problem which for me at the time, seemed almost insurmountable. Since there is something to learn in every problem of life, I decided to discover how I could benefit by this obstacle. What happened is that I forced myself to come to terms with the internal issues with which I was dealing. I found a whole new group of people to associate with, people who were much more positive and empowering than were my former friends. I learned through this experience that I was a wonderful person and had much more talent and ability than I ever saw before. I acted on what I learned, and that set the stage for my eventual success at age 19.

Take a good look at the obstacles in your path. Instead of cursing them and wishing them away, ask yourself what you can learn from your situation. How can you become a better person through them? Someone once said that we go on experiencing life's lessons until we learn what we need to learn, then we can move on. Remember, above every stormy cloud is a bright sun which never fades.

**There is something to learn
in every adversity!**

49

... THERE ARE POSSIBILITIES
IN EVERY PROBLEM.

There are two sides to every coin. The Chinese call this the Yin/Yang principle. Every negative has a positive opposite. You just have to look for it. One person's disaster will become the vehicle for another person to become wealthy. See your challenges in life as blessings in disguise and try to uncover the hidden opportunities.

During the Great Depression, not everyone went belly-up. Some people actually became rich. When you see a problem, you also need to see an opportunity. One of the fastest ways to become wealthy is to solve someone's problems or difficulties.

Many successful businesses today have been born out of someone's problem. Take the man who took surplus sawdust from the lumber mills free of charge and formulated several wood-burning products from it. He saw that lumber yards had a problem with excess sawdust. They didn't know what to do with it. He acted and began a wonderful business.

> "If it's going to be it's up to me."

51

... EVERY PROBLEM
HAS A LIMITED LIFESPAN.

Every problem will go away. Either *it* will change or *you* will. No problem is permanent. It can't be permanent because everything is in a constant state of flux; everything changes. Worry is useless. Instead, of being ready to give in, just remember that every problem has a limited lifespan. Things will get better. Seek to grow.

"Tough times never last, but tough people do."
Robert Schuller

How about communism? Or the Berlin Wall? Who could have guessed that within days, the entire Berlin Wall could be demolished. Within weeks, Communism would crumble. A problem which many people feared would plague the earth for centuries disappeared in a flash.

Look at your problem and ask "Will this matter in five years from now?" "What about next year?"

> *"Worry is like a rocking chair;*
> *it will give you something to do,*
> *but it won't get you anywhere."*

... THERE ARE NO PROBLEMS, THERE'S ONLY A SHORTAGE OF IDEAS.

Problems are not the problem. Ideas are the problem. Every single problem, challenge, or storm you face today has as its solution an idea waiting to be used. If you could only understand that the only thing standing between your current problem and the wiping away of it is nothing but an idea.

So, get your eyes off your problems and onto the solution. You may not be able to do anything about what has happened, but you surely can and should do something about finding a solution. That solution may seem like a fantasy right now, but keep in mind that the airplane was nothing but a fantasy until two brothers starting searching for ideas to solve their fantasy. Fantasies can become facts.

It was Christmas Eve. The large country church was filling up. The air was worshipful and festive. Families came from far and wide to enjoy the majestic organ playing the beautiful carol of the holidays. But suddenly a *problem* arose.

The service was about to begin when the organist discovered that a church mouse had chewed through the inner workings of the massive air chamber. With only minutes to spare, the organist quickly composed a replacement carol which he played on his old acoustic guitar.

The cords were simple and the melody sweet. That evening was the first time the world had ever heard the famous carol *Silent Night*. By focusing on the solution instead of the problem, the end result was spectacular.

... EVERYONE HAS PROBLEMS.

"The man with no shoes grumbled in the street,
until he met the man with no feet."

You're not alone. Even the most *together* people have
storms to face. In fact, the people who are winning
the most in life often have the biggest challenges in
front of them. The people who win the most in life are
often the biggest risk-takers.

Since you're not alone, why not align yourself
with others who may be facing what you are facing.
You could perhaps solve your problems together.

Upon returning from an extended international business trip, I (Dan) had an overwhelming amount of urgent telephone messages to respond to. Most of the calls were from successful business contacts or employee's who were waiting upon my direction (most were at least 10 - 20 years older than I). It was the last thing I wanted to deal with; I was tired and just wanted to relax, but I had to.

I quickly put things into perspective when I realized that this is a problem I would have given anything to have only a few years ago. I was successful and people wanted to work with me. My point is that the more successful we become, the greater the challenge. Never forget that the greater the obstacle, the greater the opportunity.

- *Principle #3*
-
-
- THE INVERSARIAN PRINCIPLE
-
-
-
- **THE POWER TO STAND ALONE**
-
-
- *"Most people think they want more money*
- *than they really do, and they settle for*
- *a lot less than they could get."*
-   Earl Nightingale
-
-
-

According to industry-wide statistics, at the age of 65, insurance companies calculate that a whopping 94% of North Americans are either dead or dead-broke. One out of a hundred are still working, and four are financially stable—in other words, they are just getting by. Out of one hundred people, only one person will be financially independent entering the Golden Years.

As Armando David Vacca says, in *The Magic of Success*, "they plan for the Golden Years but for far too many of them, it's really the Yearning Years, they are absolutely dependent upon others, even for life's essentials."

This, in the most prosperous nation on Earth, is the reality of the masses. For people who want to win at life, breaking away from the masses is an absolute must.

If you are to open your world of wealth, if you are to be truly free, you must learn to overcome your natural instincts to conform. You must become an individual. You must learn and live by *The Inversarian Principle*.

The Inversarian Principle very simply states, that you should observe the masses, and do the opposite. In business terms, that means when the masses are buying gold, you should be selling it. When they are buying real estate, you should be selling. And of course, when the masses are selling, you should be buying. But *The Inversarian Principle* goes far beyond business. When the masses are going in one direction, you should always go the opposite way. **The masses are wrong about wealth**. Most of the population is unhealthy, unhappy, and broke. What could you possibly gain by following them?

Most people are like a flock of ducks that are flying across the sky. Very seldom does a duck stop to wonder if the flock is going in the right direction. They just fall into line and follow the flock. Doesn't it make sense that a duck who follows the flock will end up exactly where the flock is headed? Of course! And when was the last time that you saw one duck change his direction, and take off the opposite way? Not too often.

We must understand, that the reality of the masses quite simply states that the masses will end up broke and dependant on others for their survival. And if we follow the flock, that's where we will end up as well. To break this pattern, we must be like the lone duck who turns in the opposite direction, and heads away from the pack. Sounds difficult doesn't it? It is! But the rewards will pay off for the rest of your life. Soon, you will be flying much higher in the sky, and enjoying the life *you* create and not the one the masses dictate.

Our Challenge

You must be an Inversarian. Observe the masses, and do the inverse. We recommend not even consulting others for important matters. By others, we mean other ducks, who don't have the results you want in life. Sure, you should get advice, but make sure you get advice from the right type of person. The criteria is results.

Why do broke people ask other broke people for opinions or advice on how not to be broke? Heck, if they had any inclination about money, do you think they'd be broke?

Why do people go to sick, overweight doctors who smoke, for medical advice? The last person who can help you to health is an unhealthy doctor. Could you learn anything from a financial planner who is not rich? Ironically, most financial planners are far from wealthy.

Believe it or not but many *motivational* speakers offer sharp tidbits of information while struggling themselves. Why would anyone ever listen to them? Be sure that you no longer rely on the advice of the masses. Remember that their advice will get you to exactly where they are going.

Many people live there lives always worried about what their family and friends think of them. Chances are, they don't think at all. That's the problem. They live their lives according to the way they think that their friends and family think that they should live. As soon as someone says, "I'm tired of being average, I want to soar with the eagles," the masses, the flock of ducks that they are with, will try to drag them down with their meaningless quacking.

Understand this—what anyone thinks of you is none of your business. At the end of the day, you must answer to yourself. At retirement, you will either have the life that you want for your family, or you will not. Others will have no solution for you at that point.

As you journey higher into the sky to join the eagles, you will find that there are two basic fears that are motivating your friends and family to try to stop you. Your family, in most cases, is motivated with good intent. They are living by the mindset of the masses, and they are not aware of their own inner strength, let alone yours. **Their fear of your failure is greater than their excitement about your success.** You must step out of the mould, despite their advice. Often times your *friends,* on the other hand, have a much more selfish motivation for trying to keep you in the flock. They live by the mindset of the masses as well. They believe that in order to get ahead in life, one is either lucky or a con artist.

> *"In fact, you may find*
> *that the key to success is luck;*
> *just ask any failure."*

The masses also spend their lives blaming others for their failure. It's the government's fault, it's the recession, it's his fault, or it's her fault. Many failures believe that the reason they are where they are is because of their lack of education, or opportunity. In truth, none of the above could be further from reality. We are responsible for our own lives. We choose our own pathway to walk by the decisions we make every day.

When you tell your *friends* that you are going to soar with the eagles, and make great things happen in your life, you may find that they are not as excited as you are about your new plans. You see, when you become successful, you will shatter the myth that they live their lives by. You instantly force them to accept responsibility for where they are in their lives, and also for where they are going.

The masses would rather live in their comfort zone. You could be a threat to their whole belief system. So, don't be surprised if when you shoot for the moon, they shoot at your heart.

Be strong! Overcome the need you might have to gain the opinions and approval of others. When you attempt to change your life, as you are doing now by reading this book, you will force opposition. You have decided to move beyond, *just getting by*. You want to better yourself.

Principle #4

CREATE A WONDERFUL SELF-ESTEEM

YOU REALLY MATTER

*"More than any other thing,
we want the conscious awareness
and experience of worthiness."*

Gerry Robert
Conquering Life's Obstacles

Why are you so popular?" asked one college student to the other. "What do you mean?" he replied. "Well, don't take this the wrong way or anything, but you are going to be our Valedictorian at graduation, you seem to have more friends than anyone on campus, all the teachers really like you, everything is positive for you even though ... (he hesitated to mention 'the birthmark')."

The other student had a huge birthmark on his face. It covered one whole side of his face. It was purple and some thought it grotesque. "The birthmark is really an advantage for me. Ever since I can remember, my dad told me that I was actually special because of the birthmark." He recalled how his father made him feel important because of the scar which other people thought was ugly.

"As a child, my father told me that God really loved me and had a special plan for my life. He wanted to be able to pick me out in a crowd. So, he sent an angel who kissed me on the face which left this mark. Now God knows exactly where I am."

This young man saw how much he mattered to God, his dad, and to himself, even with the birthmark. He turned his scars into stars, as Schuller says.

You ARE great! You weren't put here to fail. You were not designed to lose. Defeat is not part of any masterplan! You are framed for success. You are wired to shine.

You know people, as we do, who just sit, wait, and complain about how terrible life is. Refuse to be like that! Assume responsibility for your life and resist the masses who choose to live with mediocrity. You were created for success and therefore refuse the notion that you cannot make it! And make it big! Refuse to accept anything but the masterpiece you were created to be.

Understanding that you have the seeds of success within allows you to be filled with passion and enthusiasm for life. It puts you in control of any feelings of inadequacy. It helps you think creatively about solutions to life's challenges.

Some people misunderstand what self-esteem is. It is not **Narcissism** which says in essence: "Hey, ain't I enthralling." It isn't **Bragging**: "Look at how great I am." Self-esteem is the opposite of **Arrogance**: "I'm better than you." And is miles apart from **Self-centredness**: "The whole world revolves around me."

Dr. Robert Schuller said,

SELF-WORTH
is being poised instead of tense.
It's being confident instead of confused.
It's being enthusiastic instead of bored.
Self-worth is feeling successful.
More than anything,
it is being self-forgiving
instead of self-condemning;
self-respecting
instead of being self-disgusting.

YOU
MATTER!!!

Remember this: what you believe in your heart about yourself is what you are. You can change your belief. You need to believe in yourself.

Be Strong

You will control the life you live, the results you get, or someone else will. Many people do not realize that unless they consciously control their thinking, they are at the mercy of others in so many ways.

Norman Cousins, in his book, *Head First: The Biology of Hope,* shares an example of how one idea was responsible for massive illness at a football stadium in Monterey Park. A few people reported ill during the game with symptoms of food poisoning. It was discovered that all of them had purchased a soft drink at the same concession stand. The authorities feared that the syrup had been contaminated.

In an effort to protect the spectators, they made an announcement over the loudspeaker requesting that no one patronize the dispensing machine because some persons had become ill with food poisoning.

The moment this announcement was made, the entire stadium became a sea of retching and fainting people. Hundreds were rushed to local hospitals.

Why did so many people *get sick* only after the announcement was made? Someone managed to drop a suggestion into their subconscious, and without conscious thought, they all got sick.

How many times do we allow someone else to program us to have results we don't want? Take control of your thinking, don't let anyone, especially not negative thinking doom and gloom experts, cause you to think that things are poisoned. They aren't!

It was finally ascertained that the soft drinks were entirely innocent. Once this news was passed along to the patients, they got up from their hospital beds and went home.

Words were processed by the human mind in a way that made for illness and recovery. The same applies in every area of life. Choose to continue to believe *worth-building* statements about yourself. Where do we start?

Come To Terms With The Past

What effect does our past have on our self-esteem? One major reason so may people suffer with a poor self-esteem is because of the scars inflicted upon them from their past.

We doubt if any of us are not affected one way or another by our past. How many of us are totally free from its effect?

Yesterday, Today, Tomorrow

*There are two days in every week about which
we should not worry,
two days which should be kept free
from fear and apprehension.
One of these days is yesterday
with its mistakes and cares, its faults and
blunders,
its aches and pains.
Yesterday has passed forever beyond our control.*

*All the worry in the world
cannot bring back yesterday.
We cannot undo a single act
we performed yesterday.
We cannot erase a single word we said.
Yesterday is gone.*

*It's not the experience of today
that drives men mad—it is the remorse and
bitterness for something which happened yesterday
and the dread of what tomorrow may bring.*

Let us, therefore, live but one day at a time!

From A.A. Beginner's Pamphlet

Ever since I, (Dan), was a boy, I wanted to become a salesperson. As I grew older, I had to overcome the conditioning that I received as a boy from the people who ridiculed my desire to succeed in sales. I was a very shy person, everyone told me how nice I was and how quiet I was. It didn't take long for me to start living that label. Self-talk began to govern my responses to situations. When in a social setting I would respond quietly because I would tell myself "I'm a shy person." I became so shy that I thought of abandoning my childhood dream to be a world-class salesperson. I'm glad I didn't. My self-talk could have destroyed my future.

Get control of **your** self-talk. We'll address this more formally later, but to improve your self-esteem, you will need to get control of your self-talk. Self-talk is what you say to yourself about yourself. We do this all day long without even thinking about it.

- You're driving down the highway and someone honks at you as you change lanes. You look in the rear view mirror and they are obviously very upset, shaking a fist at you madly. You feel like an idiot for passing too closely.

- You ask a question at a conference. The panel has invited questions, you pose yours, and get ridiculed by one member of the panel.

- You look in the mirror and see that another diet has failed. Your diet has not only failed but you are now 17 pounds heavier than you were before you started.

- Your 17-year old son is arrested and convicted of gross negligence. You are at an office party and someone brings up the subject of children.

With all of these situations, it is very likely that most people would involve themselves in what we call *self-esteem sabotaging self-talk*. That is, there is a natural tendency for us to repeat words to ourselves that hurt our view of ourselves.

The person with a strong self-esteem learns to recover quickly from screaming motorists and embarrassing moments during question periods. They know that tearing themselves down during short-term disappointments, like when a diet fails or a child has gone temporarily astray, rarely helps matters.

God doesn't make junk!

A fundamental belief that both of us have is that we matter. We are of worth. We matter to ourselves, our friends, and family and most importantly to our Creator. Therefore, we do not allow ourselves, or anyone else for that matter, to put us down. We refuse to allow even one thought of negativity about ourselves to occupy our mind.

One of the things Jack Canfield, a leading expert in the area of self-esteem, teaches when faced with self-deprecating self-talk is to use the "Cancel/Cancel" approach. Whenever you say something negative to yourself, simply repeat the words "Cancel/Cancel" to reduce the effect those words may have on your view of yourself.

Treat yourself well – You do deserve a break today!

People with high self-esteem are easily spotted. They are the people who invest in themselves. They are the people who get massages, who get manicures, who buy nice clothes, and take the herbal wraps. These people actually believe that they are worth it. They may not be millionaires; in fact, it's not at all a money issue. It's a worth issue. It deals with how they view themselves.

If You Want To Feel Better, Then Treat Yourself Better

An interesting experience which comes to mind on the topic of treating yourself well occurred when I (Paul) was still a teenager. I treated myself well, even way back when I couldn't *afford* it.

After starting my first business, I was to pick-up the product I had merchandised. I was planning to pick it up and deliver it to my customer the same day. I was so proud that I made a sale. I got in my car, an old beat-up Volkswagen bug, which was as old as I was at the time, and headed 65 miles to the city, a feat my father felt was quite near impossible, considering the shape of this vehicle. He was right, as I was about to discover.

My sheer excitement and desire to get paid drove me forward, despite my better judgement. The car, as you probably can imagine by now, died on the highway. I was so disappointed. Fortunately, the car was a *classic*. The up-swing is that I was able to unload it for an amazing amount of $600.

It was at this point, that I decided to treat myself to something that I wanted; a new suit. I mattered to myself. I was worth the money, so I treated myself to something nice. That suit made me feel like a millionaire. When I wore it, I walked a little differently, I held myself differently, I spoke with more pizzaz—I was different.

Does the suit make the man? Hardly, we all know better than that. But I bought it and wore it as a reflection of what I thought of me. You see, everything is connected. How I looked on the outside reflected inwardly. How I felt inwardly reflected externally. I had visions of prosperity in my conscious mind. Those thoughts, or seeds, were planted in my subconscious mind and expressed themselves in prosperous ways in my life.

Mirror, Mirror On The Wall

Another technique Jack Canfield teaches is to look in the mirror before retiring and review the accomplishments of the day. Make eye contact with yourself, something many people find quite uncomfortable. Review by telling yourself all the accomplishments of the day. Don't be afraid to list even the small ones.

By repeating to yourself positive statements about yourself, you will be conditioning yourself to look for the things you have done right. The tendency of most people is to dwell on their failures and short-comings.

Canfield reports that his students have experienced everything from sheer delight to vomiting by doing this exercise. Try it; it has helped thousands of people learn to appreciate themselves more.

Notice the impact

of your words

on the quality

of your life.

Man In The Glass
(Paraphrased)

When you get what you want in your struggle for self, And
the world makes you king or queen for the day ,
Just go to the mirror and look at yourself
And see what that person has to say.

For it isn't your father or mother or spouse
Whose judgement upon you must pass,
The person who's judgement counts most in your life,
Is the one staring back from the glass.

Some people may think you a straight-shooting chum
And call you a wonderful guy,
But the man in the glass says you're only a bum
If you can't look him straight in the eye.

He's the person to please, never mind all the rest
For he's with you clear to the end
And you've passed your most difficult test in this life
If the man in the glass is your friend.

You can fool the whole world
down the pathway of life
And get pats on your back as you pass,
But your final reward will be heartaches and tears
If you've cheated the man in the glass.

- *Principle #5*
-
-
- MAKE YOUR DREAMS COME TRUE
-
-
- **GOALS FOR GREATNESS**
-
-
- *"If you don't have a dream,*
- *and if I don't have a dream,*
- *how are we going to make a dream come true."*
-                                     Mary Martin
-                        The movie, *South Pacific*
-
-

Several years ago, I (Dan), attended a *Goal Achiever* seminar given by Bob Proctor. It was not my first seminar on the subject, yet I still was not making much progress. I had heard many times of the importance of written goals, but failed to write them myself. At Proctor's seminar, he handed us a Goal Card, a pocket-size card in a plastic pouch. He stopped the seminar and refused to continue until everyone had at least one goal written on that card. I felt trapped.

It was as if I was forced into action. I wrote three goals on my card with the date that they would be accomplished. We were instructed to dream big. I did! I wrote that I wanted to own 2 real estate properties, to have a new sports car, and achieve the highest level in our sales organization. At the time, these goals seemed next to impossible. I was living in a basement apartment, delivering pizza in a 12-year old beat-up car.

Large, Passionate Goals
Produce Large, Passionate Lives

There is power in what I learned in that seminar. I looked at my Goal Card every single day. I internalized what it said. I felt like I had already attained the goals. Ten months later, while moving some boxes into our new office, I came across that original Goal Card which was misplaced for several months.

My heart stopped as I realized that every single one of the goals on that card was a reality in my life. I had the real estate properties, the Porsche, and had reached #8 out of more than 10,000 distributors in the country. It works!

Most people lack direction in their lives. They don't give any time to considering what they really want out of life. They accept what is sent their way.

Ask any poor senior citizen if they wrote out clear, measurable goals for their lives when they were younger. You can imagine what the answer will be. Now, for contrast, ask a person who reaches the golden years without any financial worries. People who reach this period of life financially fit have probably developed and stuck with a plan which included goal setting.

> *You will become*
> *as small as your **controlling** desires,*
> *as great as your dominant aspiration.*
> James Allen

Potential

We can do so much more than we give ourselves credit for. We have an incredible, unlimited resource available to us. It would shock the average person if they knew just how much they could achieve in life if they but tried, if they used what they had available. Because most people do not understand how much potential they have, they limit their aspirations to the level at which they know they can presently achieve.

It is well known that a sudden fright or danger will release every particle of energy to perform incredible feats of strength. A number of years ago, a Los Angeles newspaper published an amazing story of a woman named Francis Avita. She was a frail 100-pound woman who lifted an automobile, the portion of which weighed over 900 pounds, off the head of her brother, and saved his life. Lifting that automobile would have been an incredible feat for even a rugged 200-pound football player, but she summoned up superhuman strength upon the command of her mind.

Let yourself dream. A dream is one of the most powerful forces on the planet. Dreaming is often kicked out of us as children. Remember, it was only a dream that freed black people from slavery, it was only a dream to send a man to the moon. It was only a dream to abolish Communism. It was only a dream to cure Polio. It's only a dream today to cure Cancer and Aids. *Only* a dream? Dreams are one of the most powerful forces known to man. Remember, every major accomplishment started with a dream.

"Whatever the mind can conceive and believe, it can achieve."

Napoleon Hill

In a leading university in the United States, a study was conducted to evaluate the power of dreams and the necessity of dreams. The participants were attached to brain-wave monitoring devices. The machines would indicate exactly when the patients would begin dreaming. Whenever a person would begin a dream, they would be awakened, interrupting their thoughts and dreams. So, whenever a person would start to dream, they were stopped. The results shocked the team of doctors conducting the study. In fact, after 7 days they had to abandon the project because of the serious effects on the participants when they were not allowed to dream.

The patients became neurotic. There were signs of deep, emotional upset and imbalance due to dream depravation. Some of the patients were on the verge of insanity. The experiment was abandoned. They could not continue because the risk of the possible results were too high.

Dreaming is essential to mental health. It is even more important to the person who desires more of the good life. Anyone who truly wants to open the world of wealth must become a certified dreamer.

In grade 1, I (Dan) would sit and day-dream. My teacher had spoken to my parents about it. She said that I was a pleasant child but would not amount to much academically. They were told not to expect much from me. My parents never shared the teachers' belief with me. I found out later that when I began to take private music lessons, my parents discussed my *'problems'* with Vic Degutis, my new music teacher. Vic refused to believe such nonsense. He became my success coach teaching Paul and I to never accept mediocrity. We owe Vic a great deal! Fortunately, our parents never told me about what my teachers told them. I would have been crushed not knowing at the time that Einstein, Ford, and Edison were all similarly labeled.

There Are No Limits

There are no limits save the ones we impose upon ourselves. People have self-imposed barriers which inhibit their success. They are stopped by obstacles within their mind. A complete breakthrough would be possible by altering the smallest of things within their thinking.

How do you control the massive power of a huge circus elephant? They are giants of creatures, yet often the only thing that holds them to their stake in the ground is a tiny little chain, a chain they could effortlessly breakaway from if it wasn't for their thoughts or conditioning.

When they are born, circus elephants are tied to a stake by a huge chain. The young animal tries and tries to free himself from the chain, to no avail. Nothing seems to work. No matter how hard he pulls, nothing releases him from the chain which keeps him pinned to a certain stake in the ground. That small stake in the ground becomes his reality.

After several years of trying, the elephant stops trying. His environment convinces him that he is helpless. He gives up tugging on the chain.

The power of that conditioning overrules what we know about the strength of the mighty elephant. The same chain that held him captive at 100 pounds keeps him captive when he grows to over 1000 pounds. In his mind, the chain is more powerful than he. He conforms to his obstacles even though we know that physically, he has the strength to break away from 10 chains that size. The power of conforming to present results is phenomenal. Never settle for the chains imposed upon you.

**You have the power
to overcome your obstacles.**

Goal Achieving Tips

❑ Identify a major goal that is challenging and emotional to you. By that, we mean a goal that you can get excited about.

❑ Write the date for the attainment of your goal.

❑ Your goal will have some obstacles to overcome. It's a good idea to consider what some of those challenges will be, in advance. The first step to overcoming obstacles is identifying them.

❑ Choose a goal that you have never achieved yet. To set a goal to get a new Chrysler is not a big enough goal if you already have bought a new Chrysler.

❑ Develop a specific plan for attaining your goal.

❑ Make a list of people, organizations, and publications which might assist you in achieving your goal.

❑ Begin thinking, feeling, and acting as you will once the goal has been reached.

❑ Consider solely how the goal can be reached; refuse to accept, even for a second, that it cannot be reached. Retreat is not an option.

If you could have anything you wanted in life, what would it be? If you could do anything you wanted, or be whatever you wanted, what would you choose?

Understand this, you can have, do, or be, anything you want.

Here are some of the tools to get you to the life you deserve. Perhaps one of the strongest tools that high performance people use to continually find success in their lives is to focus very strongly on goals.

The story is told of two hungry workers having a break on a hot day in the rolling hills of Idaho. They were both sitting in the cool shade under a tree. One yawned, stretched and said "I wish I had a million apples." Where upon his friend said, "Yes, and when you get these apples, will you give me a couple hundred?" Without hesitation, the first one said, "No". "How about one hundred?" "Nope", replied the first man. "Will you give me ten?" he continued. "I wouldn't even give you one!" "How come?", he wondered. "That's because you're too lazy to wish for yourself."

You can only move ahead by letting go of old ideas. Dr. Lee Pulos, a clinical psychologist and leading authority in the area of the mind, reports that in order for change to occur, there are three basic elements that must be present: Desire, Expectation, and Imagination. Let's look at these elements.

Desire

You must want something to change. Desire is the unexpressed possibility of an idea wishing to be expressed. Don't limit your desires to what you think you can have. You must give yourself a chance to dream and to risk.

When an Egyptian shepherd boy was given charge of a flock of sheep, he was told, "The pool on the other side of the hill is for emergency only. Its water is limited, so don't use it unless other sources dry up." An extremely hot spell brought on the emergency, so the boy led his flock to the pool. Although the sheep drank from the pool all day long, the water maintained its original level.

The shepherd investigated the strange situation and made a curious discovery: the pool was fed by an underground stream. As the water was removed from the top of the pool, the underground pressure was activated into streaming upward. In other words, the pool had a constant and limitless source of supply.

A man's desire or mental powers are also limitless. "Then why," comes the logical question, "do the majority of men and women lead such limited lives?" The answer can also be found in the story of the pool: the majority of men and women never really investigate their potentialities.

They wrongly assume that what they presently do is all that they can ever do. They falsely believe that tomorrow must be as unsuccessful as today. So, they sadly accept self-limitation. And as long as people accept limitation, they will not be motivated to discover the great opportunities that lie ahead of them.

Desire
is the missing element
to open the door
to their wealth.

Expectation

You must know and expect that what you are doing will work with repetition. Never desire something you don't expect and never expect something you don't desire. A young man who experienced great misfortune confessed that he bought an astrology magazine that morning. It said that there was great danger of an automobile accident, and to be very careful.

The young man said that he was charged with fear, and shook all over when he read it. He didn't want to drive that day, but he had to go to an important audition and the only way to go was by car. He had three accidents that day, injuring one man seriously. He was suffering from shock himself, and also received some contusions and lacerations. His car was badly damaged.

"What I greatly fear has come upon me," Job said in the Bible. His great fear brought on these accidents. He planted seeds of fear in his mind, and harvested the results in his life.

Robert Schuller once asked,

"What great thing would you attempt if you knew that you couldn't fail?"

Imagination

Create mental movies of your desired goal. It's just as easy to dream for a supermarket as it is for a loaf of bread. Your goals may centre around physical, mental, monetary, or personal growth. You can work with many different goals simultaneously, but you must work through a series of steps in programming each goal for successful attainment.

A number of years ago, in a European nation, an extraordinary event occurred. Scientists were given permission to experiment on a criminal who was sentenced to death.

The criminal was informed that he was to bleed to death. He was placed on a table, with his eyes blindfolded. A small incision was made on his arm, but not deep enough to actually allow blood to flow. A small stream of warm running water was allowed to trickle down his arm into a basin, which he felt and heard distinctly.

The scientists began making remarks on the progress of the bleeding and his growing weakness. They commented on how the man was now approaching death. The man died in a short time, and suffered all the symptoms of a person who had bled to death. His subconscious mind actually created a reality based on false information from his imagination.

Action

By the end of this chapter, you will have developed a series of goals and plans for their attainment. You will be so excited about your goals that you will be empowered to achieve greatness. Let's move into constant and continuous action starting right now.

Step 1:

Make a list of every area in which you would like to see improvement. List at least 20 things you want to have, do, or be. Don't go on until you have at least 20.

Areas to consider:

- ❑ Physical
- ❑ Mental
- ❑ Spiritual
- ❑ Relationships
- ❑ Vocational
- ❑ Financial
- ❑ Toys
- ❑ Vacations
- ❑ Environmental
- ❑ Attractiveness
- ❑ Personal Breakthroughs
- ❑ Help To Others

My Personal List

Here are 20 things I want to have, do, or be:

Item   **Rating**

1. _____ ☐

2. _____ ☐

3. _____ ☐

4. _____ ☐

5. _____ ☐

6. _____ ☐

7. _____ ☐

8. _____ ☐

9. _____ ☐

10. _____ ☐

11. _____ ☐

12. _____ ☐

13. _____ ☐

14. _____ ☐

15. _____ ☐

16. _____ ☐

17. _____ ☐

18. _____ ☐

19. _____ ☐

20. _____ ☐

Today's Date _____

Name _____

Step 2:

Prioritize the list. Give each one of the 20 items an *A, B,* or *C* rating. Once this is done, select the most important *A* goal. You determine which one is most important by asking yourself, "Which one of these goals could I get the most excited about." This will be known as your *A1* goal.

Re-write it in the section below and expand upon it noting and detailing exactly how you will feel once you have achieved your goal.

Your A1 Goal

_____

_____

_____

_____

_____

_____

Step 3:

Set the date. Set a date for when you would like to accomplish this goal. At this point, don't worry as to *how* you will but rather *when* you would like to achieve this goal.

Step 4:

Dig for detail. For this goal to stick in your mind, you must be emotionally involved with it. Write a one-page description of how you will feel once you have attained the goal. Bob Proctor says you should start this step with the words, "I am so happy now that..." (then write out your goal and feelings in detail—one page minimum).

Step 5:

I'm so happy now that ...

_____

_____

_____

_____

_____

Lock into the goal. Keep your mind on your *A1* goal at all times. Refuse to ever look at your present results and think you can't achieve it.

An anxious passenger once asked the river-boat captain, "Do you know where all the rocks are?" He replied, "No, but I know where the channel is." Focus on your objective and the obstacles will disappear.

More than anything else, the growth process is the clearing away of the debris of old thought patterns, bad habits, sloppy performances, and gummy thinking. If everything you are is clogged by negativism, judgement, and body imbalance, you cannot be a channel for energy.
Stuart Wilde

You have now set one goal, your *A1* goal. This is the starting point. By the time you have finished this entire book, you will have realized many interesting and exciting things about yourself and the life you can live with the principles described in this book. You will want to go back and begin the process over again until you have fully mapped out your wildest dreams and desires.

We must have balance at this point by considering goals in each area of life. Why not set family goals, how will your relationships be? What about spiritual goals? How about physical goals? Health? How much money do you want to be worth? Where would you like to live? What *toys* would you like to have? Where would you like to travel?

The Abundant Life Is Yours For The Asking

Stella Mann said, "If you can hold it in your head, you can hold it in your hand." The powerful truth is that by keeping your mind on your desire, your desire will materialize for you. It may not be easy for you to keep your eye on what you want when what you want is so far from where you are. Never give up.

"One percent doubt and you're out!"
Mark Victor Hansen
Author, *Dare To Win*

Even though it may be *natural* to doubt your ability based on your programming, remember what Napoleon said, "I see the objective, the obstacle must give way." What that means is by locking into what we want, not the barriers to achieving it, we will unleash a powerful force to see our dreams come true. We will, by our thinking, set in motion its fulfilment.

The world is full of people who wish and wish for good. **These people wish positively but think negatively.** Because of a lack of persistence, they abandon their goals, often just before the breakthrough, and their goals and aspirations die on the vine of broken dreams.

There are countless stories of people within minutes or inches of unbelievable success who quit just a second too soon. They loose everything because they didn't *dig* that extra foot in their gold mine, or

99

they quit a *day* early before the masses got turned onto their idea or product. Keep your dreams alive.

We have discovered ten reasons why people give up too soon. We have called them the *Quitter Traps*. Never allow your goals to die away in one of these terrible traps. The main reason people don't achieve much is because they don't want much. For example, the average person spends more time planning a *vacation* than they do their *life*.

We'd like to illustrate the *Terrible Ten* by discussing our first major business venture. The end product was by all standards a smashing success. Was it easy? NO! Did we face the Quitter Traps? Yes and overcame them all. We built a business with millions of dollars in sales, with thousands of sales representatives operating in several countries. All this when we were barely out of our teens.

There is a certain apathy when it comes to life. It is rampant in our society. Ask any teenager about enjoying a prosperous life in the 90's. The answer might very well shock you. The average person settles for a life of mediocrity when super-sonic delight could be theirs for the asking. They spend more on the outside of their heads (shampoo/hair spray/hair cuts, etc.) than they do on the inside. They are so quick to reject ideas. Most people give more energy to why they can't have something than to how they can get it.

Razor's Edge

There is something known as the *Razor's Edge*. The line which separates the winners from the losers, successes from failures, is as fine as the edge of a razor. It's the smallest of improvements which make the biggest difference. In the Olympics, the winner wins by less than a hundredth of a second in many cases. The difference between the millionaire and the pauper can be just as minuscule.

The difference between a baseball player who earns $3,000,000 a year and one who earns $300,000 a year could be one extra base hit every ten times at bat. Winners go just a little further than losers. Don't be afraid to keep going the extra mile. Your success can be as close as the next page in this book.

There are ten traps which will confine you when it comes to designing a life. People try and lock you in these traps; your mother may be one of them, your Aunt Wart or Uncle Twit, as Leland Val Van de Wall says, will try and box *you* in. Resist the *Quitter Traps*. We call them the *Terrible Ten*.

THE

TEN

QUITTER

TRAPS

THE IT AIN'T PERFECT TRAP

People will get you to reject an idea or goal because there may be something wrong with it. There's something wrong with every good idea. What's wrong with these folks? Let's keep the goal even with the imperfections. So you don't have the whole solution today, so what? Our good friend, Dr. Robert Schuller, said it best:

There are no problems,
there's only a shortage of ideas.

Like any organization, ours wasn't perfect. We found out that if there are people involved, you will have imperfection. The question we asked was, "Should the imperfections cause us to stop?" For us, the answer was a resounding "No".

We started our business on a shoe-string and built it to a multi-million dollar organization. Although we had no financial backing or real credibility with others, partly due to our age and lack of success, we used our creative ability to keep going when others would have given up.

103

"You cannot

escape from a prison

if you do not know

you are in one."

Vernon Howard

THE CONFLICT TRAP

People reject goals because it might cause others to feel uncomfortable. Never deprive yourself of something you want simply because it might cause some uncomfortable conflict. There was a day when people believed in the divine right of kings, that women should not vote, that blacks were inferior, and that the world was flat. Where would the world be today if it wasn't for some healthy conflict.

As our business began to grow, we experienced incredible conflict from our peers. Our success was making them rather uncomfortable. They saw what we were doing compared to what they *weren't* doing and a gulf began to emerge between us. We had a strong temptation to stop doing what it took for us to succeed and join our friends in the warm, unthreatening comfort of mediocrity. We kept on going and became an example to our friends. Once we made the conscious decision to leave the Conflict Trap behind, our business exploded.

"Good ideas are shot down

by people who assume that the future is an

extension of the past—

The past does not equal the future."

THE FAILURE TRAP

People often get really charged up about some goal or dream, they start planning and designing things, then give up because it might fail. How sad! Every great and noble goal has a failure factor built in. If it didn't, everyone would have already attained that goal.

We almost got lost into this trap forever. We came close but won. We refused to be stopped. We had developed a rather large sales force, then something almost tragic occurred. The people who worked for us got stuck in the Failure Trap.

They could not see their way out, so, many of them quit. Almost our entire sales force left us. Rather than despair, we regrouped and developed a stronger team. We refused to abandon our goal just because, to some, it looked like it might fail. Today, with an even larger international sales team of real dedicated professionals, we are thankful that we kicked the lid off this trap and kept on going. Don't let anyone convince you to stop if you know inside that it will succeed.

"Faith is the ability to ...

See the invisible

Believe in the incredible

To get the impossible."

THE LACK TRAP

Ever wonder how many great ideas were rejected because the originator of that idea did not have the time, the money, or the manpower to bring the idea into fruition? Build and create a great life for yourself. It's all there for you. If you hold the image of your goal in your mind, you will attract everyone, and everything you need for the fulfilment of that goal. **You are like a magnet**.

If you take a tuning fork and strike the *C* note, for example, it will ring the *C* note on the piano on the other side of the room. By this unexplainable force, you attract what you focus on. Move out of lack and into plenty.

When we started our business, not only did we lack the money and expertise, we had a major time obstacle. We were teenagers with a big dream. We wanted to become wealthy, happy, and prosperous. Unlike most of our friends though, we jumped out of the Lack Trap. Dan was delivering Pizza 7 days a week and Paul was a full-time student with two part-time jobs. However, we made the time and started in business anyway.

Refuse to concentrate on lack. If your goal is big enough, the money, time, and help will all appear. Remember, the mind is like a Polaroid camera. It sees an image and produces the physical equivalent.

"Your circumstances may be uncongenial,

but they shall not long remain so

if you perceive an ideal

and strive to reach it"

James Allen

THE STRETCH TRAP

People often give up on a big goal because they would have to stretch. Stretching, for the most part, is uncomfortable so they abandon the great idea or goal. If you are to win and win big in life, you will have to learn flexibility.

Everyone has a comfort zone determined by their conditioning. The important thing is to be willing to grow and to change. Succeeding in life may require you to do things that are uncomfortable. Do it anyway! Success is the important thing, not whether you did it your way or not.

Transformation:

Seeing life the way it is,

not the way you thought it was.

THE GLOBAL TRAP

When Columbus set sail, did he have the whole picture? When you placed a deposit to buy your first house, did you know exactly where the rest of the downpayment would come from?

Most people feel they must reject dreams or goals because they don't have the whole or global picture. They aren't sure of all the composite parts, so they throw in the towel. Keep ideas floating. Give them time to germinate.

They can't grow if you yank them out of the ground simply because you don't know exactly how the whole thing will pan out.

"Don't find fault,

find a remedy."

Henry Ford

THE SUCCESS TRAP

People fear failure but many also fear success. As human beings, our very nature is to be afraid of that which we do not understand. The reason many fear success is due to the fact that they have never experienced it. You will often hear these people say that "Money will make you greedy and evil," when in truth, money has nothing to do with it. Poor and rich alike suffer from greed and evil behavior.

When I (Paul) was 20 years old, I was living in my dream home on the lake, driving my new Corvette convertible. I had half a dozen boats and was earning an outrageous amount of money, regardless of whether I worked or not. I quickly flipped into the Success Trap. I was actually afraid of my success and began to sabotage my own business. It took a lot of effort to break out of this trap. I did so by realizing that I had to shift my beliefs about myself and the way I viewed who I was. I deserved success and was entitled to all the rewards it brought to me. You do too!

"If a man hasn't discovered something

that he will die for,

he isn't fit to live."

Martin Luther King, Jr.

THE ILLEGAL TRAP

Why reject an idea just because it goes against current laws? Perhaps it's time to change the law. Remember, slavery was once illegal. People reject ideas without even considering if the law which might be in the way of their goal should be changed.

A good example is someone who wanted to build a mall on a parcel of land that was zoned for farming. Should he abandon his goal? Hardly. If people could learn to fight for what they wanted, they would enjoy so much more in life.

When the great American forefathers founded the nation, they went against many laws of their day. As a matter of fact, many were persecuted, violated, and families were threatened because they opposed the system and called for a change in the law. The Constitution of the United States of America has become the standard for Freedom throughout the world.

Government intervention is everywhere. There are many laws in place to protect the rights of the elite. The interests of certain politically charged organizations dictate many of our laws. These need to be challenged and opposed. If your dreams and aspirations are blocked by a law, then perhaps it's time to alter the law.

*"Make no little plans,
they have no magic to stir man's blood
and probably will not be realized.
Make big plans, aim high in hope
and in work,
remembering that a noble
and logical diagram
will not die."*
Daniel H. Burnham

THE IMPOSSIBLE TRAP

People are limited by their own beliefs. They give up because they perceive something is impossible. They told Edison that it was impossible to invent a light bulb, but he did it. They told Henry Ford that it was impossible to mass produce the automobile, but he did it. They told Alexander Graham Bell that he could not create the telephone, but he did it. **They told us it was impossible to succeed at our age, but we did it.** While one person is deciding why something will not work, another is making it work!

Nothing is impossible. Clear that word from your vocabulary. Thomas Edison was branded as *slow* by his teachers. He left school after only three months of formal education. He burned down his father's barn and used to sit on eggs to try and make them hatch. He was branded a misfit by society, yet he went on to become one of the greatest inventors of all time, creating over one thousand inventions including the electric light, phonograph, and movie camera.

"Man is not the sum of what he has

but the totality of what he does not yet have,

of what he might have."

Jean Paul Sartre

THE HARD WORK TRAP

Never reject an idea, dream, or goal simply because it will be hard work. Success rarely comes without it. The thing is to keep the idea alive long enough to be able to devote enough energy and/or resources towards the goal to see it come to pass.

The world of welfare and broken dreams is full of people who refuse to advance themselves because they won't work hard. If you want to move ahead and design the life you want, then stick with it and move forward one step at a time.

The issue here is abandoning your goal because of the work it will require at the beginning. It's like pushing a snowball down a hill. You push and push at the start, until you make it big enough that the snowball starts to roll on its own.

This past year has been one of the most challenging we have ever experienced. There have been more time, money, and energy spent to develop our businesses than ever before. We don't shy away from hard work, and more importantly, we don't put our dreams on hold because of it. We know that hard work, directed toward a worthy goal always reaps worthwhile results.

Principle #6

CREATE YOUR OWN DECLARATIONS OF SUCCESS

SELLING YOURSELF ON YOURSELF

"Assume a virtue and it is yours."

Shakespeare

Declarations of Success allow you to impact your Subconscious mind. The only two ways we know of to change your conditioning is through spaced repetition and emotional impact. Since whatever negative concepts you might have were put there through repetition, it follows that to replace them, you will need to use repetition as well.

Once you have identified any negative or limiting belief, you will see exactly how it has limited you. Since you want to live without self-imposed false limitations, you need to decide how you would like to be. The ultimate tool to unleashing your full potential is to write a Declaration of Success, something commonly referred to as an *affirmation*.

The Amazing Power of Belief

Olympic Gold Medalist Milt Campbell, and now one of the spokespersons for our company, is an amazing example of the power of belief. "No one ever thought I would make it," explains Campbell, "No one except for me." Milt was the last person anyone would have thought would become an athlete. He was often overlooked during sports and was picked last for the team. "I remember the time I was standing on the street with my girlfriend staring into the shopkeeper's window. Seeing my reflection, I screamed 'I am the greatest athlete in the world.' The funny thing is, at the time, I was quite scrawny and my girlfriend laughed out loud, Who are you trying to fool?"

In the beginning, Milt Campbell did not believe what seemed to be a lie. However, the more he affirmed his greatness, the more real it became in his mind. Eventually, he convinced himself that he was the greatest athlete in the world, and that's exactly what he became. He has the gold metal to prove it.

Beliefs have the power to open your world of wealth or keep you in the dungeons of poverty forever. They have the ability to unleash your potential or stifle it.

Irrational Beliefs

What belief do most of us have about the *ideal mate*? Our research indicates that we have what we call the *Cinderella Syndrome*. Most men believe that the ideal mate should be 5'5" tall, blonde hair, blue eyes, with a slim figure. The ladies believe their ideal mate should be the *Knight in Shining Armour*. He should be around 6'2" tall, brown eyes, make loads of money, be very physical, sensitive, charming, and home by 5:00 p.m. every night. These are examples of irrational beliefs. But they are widely held.

People wait forever for their Prince Charming or Cinderella. Worse yet, they leave their present mate in order to find their Prince or Cinderella. It's irrational. The truth is, there's no such thing as Prince Charming or Cinderella.

More Irrational Beliefs:

· You have to have money to make money.
· Winners are born that way.
· I'll never be wealthy.
· I could never do that.
· I can take a short-cut to success.
· It must take a long time to become rich.

125

Do you recognize any of these as a belief that you hold?   Let's work together to eliminate irrational beliefs that limit you.   You can move towards the life you want and deserve; we'll show you how.

Levels of Belief

Some people believe in themselves and some people *believe* in themselves.   Some kids believe in Santa Claus and others really believe in Santa Claus.   By speaking with some people, you can tell that they believe they will succeed, and by speaking with others, you can tell that their belief is much stronger. The reason for that is that there are four levels of belief.

In *Awaken The Giant Within*, Anthony Robbins explains that "our beliefs are generalizations about our past, based on our interpretations of painful and pleasurable experiences."   He goes on to point out: "Most of us do not consciously decide what we're going to believe; often our beliefs are based on misinterpretation of past experiences; and once we adopt a belief, we forget it's merely an interpretation." Let's examine the four levels of belief.

Belief Level 1
Hypothesis Belief

This level of belief is nothing more than a theory. This level of belief is very weak and easily abandoned.

It is rarely acted upon. Very little feeling would accompany this level. It's more like a fantasy than a belief. There would be little resistance to this level of belief.

You can easily pick this up in people. It is often called *false confidence*. A person with an Hypothesis Belief is easily swayed. They have very few facts to back up their belief. If your belief about your ultimate success is on this level, your success is just around the corner.

Belief Level 2
   Leaning Belief

This level of belief is more like an opinion than anything else. It's somewhat deeper than the first but a person would rarely risk life or limb for this belief. It might produce some action but very little. If any action would be taken from this belief, it would be feeble at best and likely not produce any measurable result.

The problem with this belief is that if it is not strong. It is highly unlikely that this person would have any facts to back up this level of belief and for sure, would have no successes to report from it. Resistance would be evident but not very strong.

Belief Level 3
Confident Belief

A confident belief is formed by supporting thoughts, feelings, and fact. A person is likely to have several facts and other data to back up this level of belief. This level of belief is different from the rest in that this level requires action. It is powerful enough to cause them to behave a certain way.

People who hold Level 3 beliefs are certain about their beliefs. These people are not necessarily closed-minded when it comes to challenging their beliefs but very close to it. They would allow discussion but would fight for this belief. They know what they know and are not easily swayed.

If you have negative Level 3 beliefs about your weight, financial destiny, or ultimate success, you will have to work hard to alter them. It can be done. We will show you how later, but it might not be easy.

Belief Level 4
Irrefutable Belief

This belief could be considered a loaded level. You don't mess with these ideas at all. This level of belief can be the very thing to open your world of wealth or the very thing which confines you to your present results.

If you have an Irrefutable Belief that you will never be a public speaker or a salesperson, chances are that there isn't enough money in the world to make you stand up in front of an audience, or to make a cold sales call.

The Difference

The thing that separates Level 4 with the rest is best described by Anthony Robbins. He says that this level "has been triggered by significant emotional events, during which the brain links up, 'Unless I believe this, I will suffer massive pain. If I were to change this belief, then I would be giving up my entire identity, everything my life has stood for, for years.'"

A person needs to hold to this belief for survival. Therefore, they would resist changing this belief like crazy. The problem is that they refuse to consider any other viewpoint. They are inflexible, rigid, and uncompromising. Any Level 4 beliefs which are positive should be maintained but negative ones must be eliminated. On the positive side, this level has produced every action required to prove the belief.

When you have developed Level 4 beliefs in a positive way, moving you towards your *A1* goal, success is certain. Nothing will stop you. The opposite is also true for negative Level 4 beliefs. They have the power to kill you.

It was a hot day in August. A man entered a refrigerated box car. By accident, the door slammed shut, locking him into the unit. He panicked. He began to feel chilled. Looking at the thermostat, he saw that the temperature would freeze him before long. During the night, he took out a pencil and wrote how after 4 hours in the cold box car, he was chilled to the bone. He wrote again a few hours later. Destitute, he feared he would soon perish. After being in the box car for 9 hours, he scribbled his last note, "I am numb from the cold. I can no longer feel my feet. Please tell my family I love them."

When authorities found him the next morning, he was dead. He died with symptoms similar to hypothermia. The sad truth is, the thermostat was broken. According to the authorities, the actual temperature could not have possibly killed anyone. His belief (Level 4) killed him. He thought it was freezing and his body materialized his fear. There is enormous power (positive and negative) in Irrefutable Beliefs.

What you want to do is identify which beliefs move you towards your end goal and which ones keep you from it.

A Case Study

Nicky believes that she cannot become a salesperson, (Level 3) her brother tries to help her by offering her a job. Since her belief is quite strong about her never being a salesperson, she refuses the offer and continues to earn a meagre salary as an office worker.

How does Nicky shake this Level 3 Belief? First, she must identify it as a disempowering belief. That is, this belief will likely prevent her from earning the money she desires to earn. Secondly, she needs to question the validity of that belief. If you question long enough, you begin to doubt; doubt opens the door to possibility. Thirdly, associate massive pain to holding the belief. If you would like to replace the belief then get your brain to see all the pain associated with holding onto it.

In Nicky's case, she could see herself losing a life of luxury afforded to top producing salespeople. She could get herself to link the old belief with a life of living paycheck to paycheck. If she did it long enough and internalized the link, ultimately the fear of pain would cause the belief to change. Fourthly, replace negative or weak beliefs by raising empowering beliefs to Level 3 or 4.

Do more research about the results that you would get if you adopted the empowering belief. In Nicky's case, she could speak with professional and successful salespeople to better understand the rewards of a winning sales career. She could meet with other people who thought they would never enjoy sales and ended up winning sales awards. This would bolster or raise the belief she wanted to instill.

A belief is simply a feeling. The degree of intensity of that feeling of certainty will determine the Level of the belief. Thoughts, feelings, emotions, facts, data, and personal experience increase the level of certainty.

Action Note

Make a list of your beliefs, then rate which level they are presently and finally, what level you would like them to be. On the left side, list all the beliefs you hold which would limit you in some way. Here are a few limiting beliefs:

- ❑ My family isn't wealthy.
- ❑ I'm a loser.
- ❑ I'm not good looking.
- ❑ I'm shy.
- ❑ I'm not good with people.
- ❑ Only bad things happen.
- ❑ I'm unlucky.
- ❑ I'm dumb.
- ❑ I m' not a winner.
- ❑ My life is outside of my control.
- ❑ I don't matter.
- ❑ I hate myself.
- ❑ I'm too fat / skinny / young / old.

My Empowering Beliefs

Now, list your freeing, empowering beliefs, rate their level of intensity, then note where you plan to take them. Limiting beliefs should be lowered in intensity level and empowering beliefs should be heightened.

Intensity   **Freeing, Empowering Beliefs**

❑ _____

_____

❑ _____

_____

❑ _____

_____

❑ _____

_____

❑ _____

_____

❑ _____

_____

❑ _____

_____

Here are a few empowering beliefs:

- ❑ I can do it.
- ❑ I will succeed.
- ❑ I am capable and lovable.
- ❑ I always ask for help.
- ❑ I'm not afraid to try.
- ❑ I pick myself up quickly after downfalls.
- ❑ Everything I do turns to gold.
- ❑ I will conquer all my obstacles.
- ❑ I deserve wealth.
- ❑ I am unstoppable.
- ❑ I love others and they love me.
- ❑ I can do anything I set my mind to.
- ❑ If it's going to be, it's up to me.
- ❑ I control my own destiny.

The power to open your world of wealth, be it emotional, financial, spiritual, relational, lies in your ability to strengthen or lessen the Levels of Beliefs in the gamut of your belief system. Knowing which ones you want to increase and which ones to decrease is the first step in this process.

Dr. Walter Staples opens his book, *Think Like A Winner,* with 10 core beliefs that are common to all peak performing men and women. It's a powerful and very accurate list. As you read Dr. Staples list below, ask yourself, "Which of these core beliefs do I presently have fixed in my subconscious mind?" Also, ask yourself, "Which of these beliefs should I work on?"

Staples' Core Beliefs

1. Winners are not born, they are made.

2 The dominant force in your existence is the thinking you engage in.

3. You are empowered to create your own reality.

4. There is some benefit to be had from every adversity.

5. Each one of your beliefs is a choice.

6. You are never defeated until you accept defeat as a reality, and decide to stop trying.

7. You already possess the ability to excel in at least one key area of your life.

8. The only real limitations on what you can accomplish in your life are those you impose on yourself.

9. There can be no great success without great commitment.

10. You need the support and cooperation of other people to achieve any worthwhile goal.

Now, pick one belief from this list which needs improvement and begin to fix that belief deep within your mind for the next 90 days. It will change your life!

Your results show what your beliefs are. If you are unhappy with your results change your beliefs. Our favourite from this list is #3, "You are empowered to create your own reality." You are! You really are!!! Create a magnificent one for yourself.

Declarations

Imagine you were a farmer, and after seeding your whole field, you realized that your hired hand had by accident loaded rock salt into the seeding machine, thinking it was seed. Knowing this, how much time would you spend watering, fertilizing, and weeding your field. The answer is obvious. Many people believe they have as little chance of succeeding in life as a farmer does of reaping a harvest from rock salt.

Be like a farmer who knows his seeds will yield a bountiful harvest. How? Work the field of your mind by using *Declarations of Success*.

Rules For Creating Powerful Declarations

Rule 1

Start with the words "I am...." This is a statement *to* yourself, *about* yourself.

Rule 2

Stay positive. Only use words that you want your mind to picture. If I say "the dog is not chasing the cat", chances are you will see the dog chasing the cat. That is because your brain has a hard time with the negative.

The negative expression would say, "I'm not a failure." The positive expression would say, "I'm a total success." When it comes to affirmations, say it positively.

Rule 3

Write only in the present tense. Be sure to write your Declaration in such a way as if it is happening now. Create a picture as if you were describing the completed result over the telephone to someone. Words like, "I should/someday/soon/will" are ineffective when it comes to reprogramming the mind. Say it as if it were fact. For example, **"I am** earning $57,000 per year. **I am** driving a blue Buick Park Avenue."

Rule 4

Keep them short.

Rule 5

Be specific. We have seen affirmations using words like *lotsa money*. No one knows what *lotsa* is. Decide exactly what would you like to see accomplished and write that precisely.

Rule 6

Use feeling words, (e.g.: happily, proudly). This whole exercise is to engage your emotions into the goal achieving process. Be sure to use words which stir up feelings for you.

Action Note

WITHOUT FAIL
read your Declarations of Success
every morning just as you awaken,
and again every evening
just before you drift off to sleep.

I (Dan) remember in high-school, walking down the hall and running into Moe Targon, my gym teacher. "How are you, Dan?" he asked. "Pretty good", I replied. "Only pretty good? What's wrong?" "Nothing is wrong." I replied. He continued, "You are alive, healthy, and live in a free country, things should be terrific." I responded, "I guess they are."

That day, I learned the power of Declarations. I learned that by saying that I am terrific, I confirm my belief about myself and my world. It is a declaration we can use several times per day. If you are like me, you may feel awkward the first few times you say that things are *terrific*; do it anyway.

- *Principle #7*
-
-
- DISCOVER THE POWER
- OF ASSOCIATION
-
-
- **MAXIMIZING RELATIONSHIPS**
-
-
- *"If you lie down with dogs,*
- *you will get up with fleas."*
-   Bobby Charleton
-   Master Motivator
-
-
-

C harlie Tremendous Jones says who you will be in five years is directly proportionate to the books you read and the people you meet. This is true. This principle will help you see the need to alter the people you are in contact with and assist you to make the necessary changes which will help you open your world of wealth.

Our research indicates people associate with people who are generally like they are. Welfare recipients are with other welfare recipients. Wealthy people associate with other rich people. The reason for this has to do with comfort. Someone making $25,000 is not very comfortable with someone making $250,000 per year. If they could overcome this discomfort, not only would they learn a lot from the higher producer but they would tend to move in that direction.

Why not create a list of influential people from whom you could learn something? Make an appointment to meet with them. Tell them that you would like to better yourself and that you would like to formulate a few questions and meet with them for a few minutes to *pick their brain*.

Everyone who is not rich should buy a millionaire lunch. One of the fastest ways to improve your life is to associate with people who have the results you want. Look for qualities in others that you would like to assimilate into your own life. For example, if you would like to be more loving, find people whom you admire in this area and spend some time with them. You will find that their beliefs and qualities will rub off on you.

> *"A single conversation with a wise person,*
> *is worth a month's study of books."*
> Old Chinese Proverb

Here are five suggestions we use to develop power associations:

1. Create a list of power associations.

This list has two parts. First, list the qualities you would like to possess and learn more about. Secondly, list the people you would like to meet who display such qualities. Your list could look something like this:

Characteristics I would like to develop:

- Honesty
- Salesmanship
- Wealth building
- Success Image
- Loving
- Charitable
- Power and Influence
- Communicator

People whom I would like to meet who have these qualities:

- Robert Schuller
- Norman Vincent Peale
- Mark Victor Hansen
- Gerry Robert
- Bob Proctor
- Mother Theresa
- The butcher on the corner
- The bank manager

2. Plan an approach.

Give some consideration to how you will approach these people. For some people, letters work better than a telephone call. Most people are willing to lend a hand. All you have to do is ask!

Once you have identified whom you would like to associate with, we suggest the following approach. Let them know briefly who you are and that you would like a few minutes of their time to learn more about winning in life. Inform them about why you admire them and what you hope to gain from your meeting.

3. Be attractive.

By this we mean, dress sharply, and smile. Have a wonderful attitude. One of the things that people do wrong when they approach someone in this fashion, is that they spend forever discussing their whole life story.

Keep in mind that you are there to hear from them. They are the ones who should be speaking, not you. Ask a question, then listen. Good communicators listen more than they speak. Try to always listen twice as much as you talk.

Here are a few questions which might help:

- What makes you so successful?
- What advice do you have for someone like me?

- Can you recommend any books that have helped you?
- What organizations do you belong to?
- If you could live your life over again, what would you do differently?

4. Be brief.

Successful people will respect you if you respect their most precious commodity—time. Tell them you would like to meet them for 45 minutes but plan to leave in 30 minutes.

5. Always follow-up.

The easiest thing is to send a brief thankyou note for spending time together. Share with them how they helped. They will remember you for a long time because very few people would actually do this very effective action step. People appreciate being recognized for sincere contribution.

We also recommend, where appropriate, to continue the relationship. The best thing most people can do is completely change their associations. By this, we mean alter the group of people you spend time with, either friends or colleagues.

A mother eagle sat high atop a great redwood tree, warming her eggs. As expected, one of the eggs hatched and out there emerged an eaglet. It cried for nourishment as the mother flew off to fill the order. While away, the other eggs began to hatch. Before

145

long, there was plenty of hussle and bussle in the nest. In all the commotion, an egg was nudged out of the nest.

It fell and landed in a soft bush below, cracking open. A baby eagle emerged and greeted the day. He had no idea where he was, how he got there, nor what to do next. At that very time, a family of prairie chickens passed by. They invited the newborn eaglet to join and he fell quickly into line.

Many years passed and he was raised by the prairie chicken family. The baby bird grew into a mighty eagle. Since he'd been raised by prairie chickens, he found his food by scratching the ground for seeds and bugs. He walked quickly from one place to another, keeping his long wings folded close to his body. Often he stood in the open field and looked up into the sky where a mighty eagle swooped and soared through the heavens. How he envied the eagles. He'd give anything to be able to fly.

He asked his brother about the bird in the sky and his brother told him: "That's the eagle, the king of birds. Don't even think about him. We're just lowly prairie chickens. We could never fly like that."

So the bird went back to pecking the ground for food and walking in a line, folding his wings back. Eventually, this eagle died—never having taken flight. He died as a prairie chicken. He never dreamed he was an eagle.

Move Towards Success Through The Group Dynamic

It is a well-known fact that the giants of our day, and those of days gone by, participated in what we refer to as a *Group Dynamic*, sometimes referred to as Master Mind group. People such as W. Clement Stone, Napoleon Hill, Henry Ford, Abraham Lincoln, and countless others, were all involved in this practice.

The purpose of Group Dynamic is to increase our ability to think, create, and reason. By working together in this format, all of the people involved have the opportunity to solve problems, add to business ideas, and think of ways to turn ideas into reality.

When two or more people come together in the spirit of harmony, their minds begin to work together. Science is still unable to explain what happens. The group's ability to think becomes exponentially greater, based upon the number of people involved.

A group of batteries hooked up together will produce more energy than a single battery, and the amount of energy produced is proportionate to the number of batteries hooked together. The group dynamic works the same way. When you create your Group Dynamic, it is important that you only involve positive people who have a sincere interest in helping each other. If there is not harmony with all involved, it will break the flow of energy, just like unhooking one battery. This blending of mental powers can be compared to the blending of physical power. One person can push a car. Ten people can lift a car.

One person will act as the leader of the group, and should open the meeting with a prayer or a few minutes of quiet time, preparing the group for inspiration. The length of the meeting should be defined before you begin. A strict schedule should be set up so that everyone involved gets an equal amount of the group's time, to work on their problem or idea. A nominal amount of time should be invested in explaining the topic of discussion, leaving the bulk of the time allotted for the group to work together on a solution.

Although the Group Dynamic principle which we have just explained seems very simple, do not underestimate its power. There is something to be said about working together with others, and helping your fellow human beings.

As you can see, success will be amplified many times over for you if you don't try to do everything yourself. Take the time to glean all the knowledge and experience you can from others through association with those who are positive, successful role models.

Remember, people are all too happy to help you with your goals if you only take the time to ask them for their assistance. The output from several minds working in unison will far exceed the sum total of each on its own.

Discovering the power of association can be one of the most exciting and personally developing exercises available to you in your endeavors. Following the rules of developing power association coupled with the steps of the group dynamic will ensure that you will fly with the eagles.

Don't try to 'reinvent the wheel'.
Rather, spend your time learning from those
who can save you so much time, effort, and
heartache having already broken the trail for you.

Principle #8

ACCEPT RESPONSIBILITY

NEW WAYS TO WIN

*"If the end brings me out all right,
then what is said against me won't matter.
If the end brings me out wrong, then ten angels
swearing I was right would make no difference."*
Abraham Lincoln

In a far off land, high in the hill-tops, there lived a wise man. People would travel from miles around, travelling day and night, just to speak to the old man. Many had great philosophical questions, many sought advice, but many would also come to try and trick the old man with a riddle. The old man had a reputation that he had never been stumped by a riddle. One day, as the old man was rocking in his chair reading ancient literature, he heard a knock on the door. When he answered the door, he was astonished to find two young boys. He invited the boys inside.

The one boy had his hands cupped, while the other boy looked on with excitement. "Old man", said the boy, "we have a question for you". "Speak, my son", replied the old man. "In my hands, I have a baby bird. Is that bird alive, or is that bird dead?" The old man paused for a brief period, and then replied, "Son, if I tell you that the bird is alive, you will crush it and it will be dead. If I tell you that the bird is dead, you will open your hands and let it be free. You see, the decision is in your hands, and

the responsibility is yours."

We can never go wrong by doing our best. The bottom line in life is that we are responsible for where we are and where we are going. You hear it every day; people blaming others for where they are in life. It's always someone else's fault. One of the best things we can ever learn to do is to accept responsibility for our lives. In fact, accepting responsibility is one of the key factors that maturity is measured in.

Maturity is not measured in age. Many adults are very immature. Yet, a teenager who has learned to take responsibility for his or her actions, decisions, and results, has truly learned one of the most important lessons of adulthood. True leadership is also measured in a leader's ability to accept responsibility for whatever happens to his or her team, organization, company, or country. Followers have the habit of passing the buck to the next person. They look for the fault in others rather than in themselves.

Many years ago, President John F. Kennedy was involved in a situation that did not work out as he and his advisors had planned. In fact, it was quite a failure for the United States as a country. Kennedy easily could have blamed the affair on his advisors, on political factors, or on other world leaders, but he chose to accept responsibility himself. He made a great statement of leadership.

You have so much more potential than you can even imagine. Petite women have lifted cars, rich people have given everything away to serve as missionaries, poor people have become billionaires, uneducated farmers have solved world crises. Anything is possible if you can persist and know how to get the most from yourself.

Put Yourself Totally On The Line Every Time

The first element in putting yourself totally on the line every time you do something is to be wholly committed to yourself and to your activity. Until you are committed, there is room for hesitancy—that chance to draw back from progress; the result is always one of ineffectiveness. Steadfast resolution to put behind your effort everything you have emotionally, mentally, and physically without hesitation, is of critical importance. You must not let any fear of losing even enter your mind.

Failure does not exist! You may have some difficulty in rationalizing this concept, but all that is necessary is to view it from a different perspective than that with which you have been conditioned all your life.

There are
NO
failures, only lessons!

Therefore, regardless of the outcome of your efforts, you still gain experience. You may not attain exactly what you had previously expected, in precisely the manner you intended, but you do gain knowledge. You still come out a winner with success to build upon even further in the future.

Just remember never to be afraid to lose, because in reality, you aren't really losing at all. As long as you never give less than your best effort, the absolute minimum you will gain is self-satisfaction in having done your best.

Many times, we are afraid to take responsibility for our failures because failures often times hurt. As a society, we have been wrongfully taught that it is failure is negative. Great achievers know that that is not so. Thomas Edison tried 10,000 times before he discovered an electric light bulb that would work. While some would say he failed 10,000 times, Edison looked at it differently. He said that he had discovered 10,000 ways that light bulbs would not work.

Henry Ford said "Failure is the opportunity to begin again more intelligently." Babe Ruth is the Hall of Fame baseball player with the record for the most home runs, 714. He also has the world record for the greatest number of strike-outs, 1330. Do you think there might be a correlation? Of course. If you fail twice as much, you will generally succeed twice as much, as long as you don't quit. Incidentally, which of Babe Ruth's records do you think he is known best for, his home runs or his strike-outs?

In the event that you do not attain your original goal immediately, refuse to make excuses. Reaffirm your commitment to work longer and harder with a positive attitude and you will ultimately attain your goal. There is a right time and place for everything.

Never Surrender

Never throw in the towel, even against impossible odds or bad luck. There are a host of words in our language that you should concentrate on eliminating from your daily thought: words like can't, impossible, hopeless, futile, carry a negative connotation that work ardently against your success unless you eradicate them from your conscious thought. Even the word *luck* denotes the existence of something that we have considerable difficulty defining. The reason for that is because it really does not exist. Everything in our lives happens for a reason. Although we don't always realize it, there are thoughts in our minds that actually bring about what happens to us, and *luck* has nothing to do with it.

155

More often than not, our desire to give up emanates from a lack of self-confidence or self-esteem. Self-confidence grows with successful accomplishments, even if only small ones, building one on top another.

An achiever accepts the responsibility to make it happen, no matter what it takes. We can learn from a baby who, when learning to walk, persists until he or she learns to walk.

When was the last time you heard of someone who became too frustrated learning to walk as a child, and decided to crawl for the rest of their life? Obviously, it doesn't happen, but some people have less sense than a baby. They approach a task with an *I'll try* attitude.

The word *try* is really an invalid word. Let me give you an example. Try to pick up a chair. Grab hold of the chair and try to lift it. We said, just *try*. Now, you are probably thinking, "how do I carry out the act of trying without actually lifting the chair?" You see, you can't. In reality, you either lift the chair or you don't. There is no such thing as trying to lift the chair. It's one or the other. Catch yourself the next time you hear that word come from your mouth. Either commit or don't. There is no in-between.

In the movie *Star Wars*, Yoda asked Luke Skywalker to commit to winning the battle with the force of darkness, Darth Vader. Luke said, "I will try". Yoda responded with "Luke,...either you do or do not, there is no try".

Persist until you achieve your results, and believe that the world is on your side, because it is. Don't allow fear of failure to immobilize you. Fear is a movement of your mind which creates what you expect.

What You Fear, You Will Attract, And What You Experience Is What You Expect

We can put fear of failure behind us by doing the things we fear. Do the things you fear, and you will control fear. By refusing to back down, refusing to quit, and persisting in achieving your results, you will succeed.

When you are feeling down and ready to quit, step back and take another look at your situation for a moment; view it from the point of a challenge. What you are attempting may not be that conventional, but you must challenge the conventional in order to succeed. You need the perseverance to do as you dream because you are betting on yourself. You must have an unreasonable passion—virtually an obsession—for being your best. After all, an obsession is the persistent, disturbing preoccupation with an often unreasonable idea. Break away from convention and you will be amazed at how you will *always* attract all the help you need.

Never Turn Against Yourself
During Tough Times

The reality of life is that things don't always go perfectly for all of us, all the time; accomplishing our goals can entail a lot of hard work and difficulties. That's what being human is all about, and it's perfectly normal.

The important thing is to never put yourself down in such situations and to maintain—even reinforce—a strong, positive attitude. Perseverance is one of the most important principles until you eventually get yourself back on the right track. If you use up your energy fighting yourself, you won't have any left to battle your opponent. That opponent may be anything from a particular person, as in a sport, to overcoming something you find particularly difficult.

Be Prepared Mentally

No athlete expects to enter a competition without first having spent considerable time and energy in practice. The same applies to whatever you want to do in attaining your goal. Contrary to common belief, practice should encompass about ten percent physical effort and ninety percent mental preparation. Do whatever is necessary to get your mind focused. Practice with the same intensity and emotional commitment that you'll generate in the real situation.

Being mentally prepared helps accomplish numerous things simultaneously. It not only contributes to the building of positive accomplishment but also helps overcome the obstacles you will no doubt encounter along the road to success. To develop a never ending list of affirmations which you can implement immediately, whenever necessary, it helps to be aware of some typical limiting statements in advance of your being faced with them. How often in the process of attaining your goal have you been bombarded with some of the following comments?

You can't always have a job you can enjoy.
You're dreaming; get real.
Don't expect what you know you can't have.
You don't know how to do that.
You don't have enough education.
You don't have sufficient experience.
You aren't smart enough to do that.
Sure, I'll believe that when I see it.
Just who do you think you are anyhow?

Keep Your Perspective

When getting the most from yourself starts producing incredible, positive results, it is all too easy to be so immersed in all the detailed activity that you lose sight of the overall picture. Participating with that sort of intensity is an absolute necessity for success.

However, you must occasionally take on the role of a spectator for a moment, step outside this fervour

159

of activity, and take a look at yourself. This process will give you a brief break in the intensity, permit you to recharge your *batteries* with ever-expanding energy and enable you to re-enter the process more intensely. The process of retaining perspective on your activities is a very powerful tool for managing stress and maintaining emotional balance.

There are a number of proven methods that you can implement to accomplish this *stepping-out* process. Combining them in different ways simultaneously can have an even greater positive impact.

• Exercise

Take some time each day to exercise both your body and mind. Go for a walk once a day. Purchase some exercise equipment to use at home. If you prefer, join a health club and participate in some aerobic and muscular exercising activities.

• Work

Try avoiding the temptation to become a *couch potato* if you are prone to such enticement. The possibilities to work at something other than or in addition to your regular job are endless. The change in mental and/or physical stimulation can be unbelievably positive and inspiring. Get those creative juices flowing in your mind; after all, the more you work your mind, the stronger it becomes.

· Relationships

Take some time out on a regular basis to communicate effectively with a close friend, your spouse, your children, a relative, or mentor. Discuss your current activity and goal, and use this person as a sounding board to help verify how well you are maintaining your perspective.

· Solitude

The human body can handle heightened activity effectively only so long without the need to benefit from one of the easiest stepping-out activities, that of active relaxation. The important point here is that to be most effective in your heightened activity, you must provide yourself with adequate and equally effective rejuvenation activities.

"The credit belongs to the man
who is actually in the arena,
whose face is marred
by dust, sweat, and blood.
Who strives valiantly, who attempts,
and comes short, again and again,
who knows the great enthusiasm,
the greater devotion
and spends himself in a worthy cause,
who at the best
knows the triumph of high achievement
and at the worst, if he fails,
at least knows he failed daring greatly,
so that his place shall never be
with those cold and timid souls
who know neither victory nor defeat."

General Douglas MacArthur

Principle #9

THE MASTER PRINCIPLE

THE POWER OF ACTION

"There is nothing brilliant nor outstanding
in my record, except perhaps this one thing:
I do the things that I believe ought to be done...
and when I make up my mind to do a thing,
I act!"

Theodore Roosevelt

We are privileged to have staff around us who live out those words of wisdom from Roosevelt. Before I can blink, Andra, one of our associates, has finished jobs she knows must be done. We never have to worry about her taking action.

When we turn to Peter, we can completely relax about what needs to be done because we know he will act and act decisively to complete what needs to get done. The same is true for all our team. We expect action, if action is required.

Mark, who is in charge of our public relations, can handle even the most difficult situations swiftly and with grace. He knows how to make things happen. Action is the buzz-word of our team!

Without action, everything is theory. Achievement of any kind requires movement. The masses prefer to deliberate, cogitate, and commiserate instead of act, and it shows in their results.

There are two main reasons people refuse to act. First, people fail to take action because they lack a significant goal or purpose which will catapult them to action. Mother Theresa, on a visit to Lebanon, drove right into the war zone to free needy sick children. She has purpose and that purpose moves her to do something. Purpose raises you above all circumstance. What is your purpose? What is motivating you? What is your goal? What do you want to have, do, or be?

The second major roadblock to action is fear. Don't be afraid to be afraid. Fear is part of being human. We still get scared. Big deal; move on anyway. Something more important than fear drives us—our goals.

> *"Do the thing you fear most*
> *and you will control fear."*
> Bobby Charleton

Remove these two obstacles and action will follow almost automatically. Cultivate the habit of action. If you want something to happen, make it happen!

This whole book is nothing more than knowledge unless you act. Refuse to be counted among the brilliant people who never make a change in their results because they forget the most important step—ACTION.

The world is full of people who think they know how to open a world of wealth. They read the material and could probably even write a book like this one. Since they can remember it, write it, and repeat it, they think they know it. You will know it when you do it!

> *We are paid,*
> *not for what we know,*
> *but for what we do*
> *with what we know.*
> Peter Webster
> International Promoter

Action - The Master Principle

The sole objective of this book is to cause you to move confidently in the direction of your goals. The main thing we want you to do is act. We have accomplished little with this book if we have failed to cause you to do something with the material you have just read. We are proposing that you find two habits which, if done every single day, would definitely open your world of wealth.

What two things could you begin today to move you in the direction of your goals? What two actions, if done every day, would make you proud and cause you to have the life you truly deserve? For example, you would win if you decided to spend 20 minutes every day filling your mind with positive material— reading books or listening to motivational tapes.

List two habits you know will lead you to your goal.

Education does not mean teaching people
what they do not know.
It means teaching them to behave
as they do not behave.

John Ruskin

167

Two Actions

I will act on two action steps for no fewer than 90 days from today. I will do the following action steps every day whether I feel like it or not.

I commit to act!

Action Step 1

_____

_____

_____

_____

Action Step 2

_____

_____

_____

_____

Signature   **Date**

Our Commitment To Help You

Here's what you must do. Write out these two actions and mail us a copy of the actions you will take. Mail to:

Destiny Seminars International Inc.
276 Kingsbury Square, Suite 104
Lake Tahoe, Nevada
89449

Note: Be sure you write your return address clearly on the outside of the envelope.

We will not read the action steps, but we would like to mail that same letter back to you in 60 days. This will build some accountability for your action steps. We want to see you act. Nothing happens without action. We are committed to your success. We want you to promise to do this. It will really help you. Decide to do it right now. Don't worry about the exact wording of your action steps. Just begin today and send us your copy.

There is no real big secret to anyone's success. It has little to do with intelligence, special skills, or gifts. It has little to do with education. We are a good example. It has little to do with working hard or receiving an inheritance.

Act by smashing through the adversities which will try to stop you. People are often discouraged because of unpleasant or unexpected challenges. The reason you'll need to act in the face of adversity is because if you plan to succeed, you will without a doubt run head on into adversity. There is no success without challenges.

Be aware that perseverance is your ally during the tough times. Stick it out just a little bit longer. Continue to move forward even when problems seem insurmountable. Your success will be in direct proportion to your willingness to keep going in spite of the obstacles. If you really want to have, do, or be something special, refuse to quit.

After reading a book like this, and we challenge you to action, there may be a feeling of being overwhelmed with everything. Act anyway. Far too often, people will end up doing nothing because they get somewhat overloaded. They can get so excited about the world of wealth that they get lost in *dreamland*.

If you are not acting on the information in this book, you will tend to feel frustrated. In the middle of the battle, things can look crazy when they aren't. A brief time out to evaluate the situation can be the best thing to get you back on track. What this might do is get you to narrow your focus again. You can't do everything, so just decide to do something. The only way to eat an elephant is one bite at a time.

Whatever you do, start! Even if it's only one thing, begin. You can't get to second base when your feet are stuck on first. People have such a hard time with this *Master Principle* of action because it calls for change. Shaking people out of their *comfort zones* is never fun. **Change is essential if we want to open the world of wealth.**

The irony is that people are constantly changing anyway. Nothing ever stays the same. You are getting richer or you are getting poorer. You are developing or deteriorating. Don't be fooled, you will change whether you like it or not.

Why not take control of the change process by selecting actions and habits which will take you in the direction of YOUR goals and not those of society, advertisers, or the media.

The time to begin is right now. There is only *right here* and *right now*. The time is never *perfect* to begin acting on this information. People will put off beginning by creating the myth that they'll begin once everything is right. There's no such thing!

The time to start this program is today, right now! Calculate how many weeks you actually have to live, assuming you make it to age 75. You may be very surprised at your limited amount of this precious resource we call *time*. The only time you can be certain of is called TODAY. The only time you have today is called NOW.

If you want to make something happen, then act. Make it happen starting this very minute. Don't delay! Today is the day to use the Principles and open your world of wealth.

The Rabbit and the Fox

At the edge of the Great Forest stood a huge Rosewood tree which overlooked a dramatic life and death tale. It began when a fox named Wilbur decided to venture out on his own, away from his friends. He was tired of being a follower and wanted to make it on his own. His spirits were keen and his senses sharp as he trotted across the meadow.

On the other side of the field, Chester, the rabbit, was deciding to make a move of his own. He began hopping off, on his own. It wasn't long before Wilbur, the fox, spotted Chester.
The chase was on.

The fox chased the rabbit wildly across the meadow. It was a mad run and each time Wilbur's teeth were about to close in on Chester, the rabbit would dart in a different direction. The chase went on for what seemed like hours as all the other rabbits and foxes cheered on.

Finally, Wilbur the fox, having almost tasted victory, gave up in total exhaustion. The rabbit returned to his group in the midst of wild cheering and jubilation. He was branded a hero and given a place of honor among his fellow rabbits. Everyone among the rabbits seemed overjoyed.

Meanwhile, Wilbur, with his tail between his knees and head bowed in humiliation, rejoined his group. His fellow foxes jeered him, laughing at him wildly. He couldn't even catch the lowly rabbit. He was the laughing-stock of the group.

This went on for quite some time, until finally, Wilbur couldn't take it any longer. Addressing the group, he said, "You can laugh all you want, but none of you understand what was really happening out there today. You see, I was just running for my dinner. The rabbit was running for his life."

Run for your life, not just your dinner.

ABOUT THE AUTHORS

DAN AND PAUL MONAGHAN

By age 21 and 23, Dan and Paul Monaghan had built a 14 million dollar empire. With a sales force of over 3,000 strong, their organization stretched across four countries. They were driving their dream cars, and had amassed a large real estate portfolio. By most people's standards, they had achieved more by their early twenties than most do in a lifetime.

Two years earlier, they were more than broke. Coming from a simple family, their father a janitor, and their mother a part-time nurse, their dreams of financial freedom to most seemed impossible. While delivering pizza's and doing odd jobs, these possibility thinkers, Dan and Paul, plotted their course for the future. A course that would bridge the gap between simple roots and great dreams. The rest is history.

The Monaghans believe that success in anything can be attained by understanding and implementing some simple principles and having a formula to follow. They recognize that the world would be a better place if everyone was moving towards becoming the best they could be. Dan and Paul have simplified the principles that worked for them and as a result of sharing these with others, they have inspired millions internationally through television, radio, appearances, as well as newspapers and magazine articles. They have been featured on television, in magazines across North America.

As favoured speaking personalities, they have been in great demand. they have spoken in front of thousands, and trained with some of the top trainers in the world. They have appeared on several bestselling audio and video training programs.

The Monaghans are the Founders of Destiny Seminars, a worldwide organization dedicated to personal growth through the development of superior personal development programs. This company grew from their sense that in order for people to experience more of the good life, they would need to grow from the inside out. Destiny Seminars is poised to impact the world in an unprecedented way.

If you would like to know more about Destiny Seminars please feel free to contact the World Head Office.

Destiny Seminars International Inc.
Canada: 5915 Airport Rd., Suite 700
Mississauga, Ontario L4V 1T1
Tel: (905) 678-7722 • Fax: (905) 678-7242

USA: 276 Kingsbury Square, Suite 104
Lake Tahoe, Nevada 89449